SHAMANIC HEALING

Norman W. Wilson PhD

SHAMANIC HEALING

ZADKIEL PUBLISHING

ISBN: 978-1-78695-761 0

Zadkiel Publishing
Is an Imprint of Fiction4All
www.fiction4all.com

This Edition Published 2022

Cover Design by
Stephen R Walker Designs
www.srwalkerdesigns.com

Based on an original design by Dr. Omar Lopez

PHOTOS OF TOOLS AND CRYSTALS BY
Suzanne V Wilson Photography
Herb Photos by Pixabay

DISCLAIMER

There are no guarantees that any of the procedures described herein will work. Before following the use of any of the suggested procedures always consult your medical doctor. Persons under the age of eighteen should not attempt these activities. Please remember you are responsible for how you use the information contained in this book.

Norman W Wilson, PhD
03/2022

APPRECIATION

I am deeply appreciative for the faith, the help, and the encouragement, each of the following so generously gave me: Omar Lopes, Stephen Walker, Patricia Bloom, Stuart Holland, and, Suzanne V Wilson, my wife.

DEDICATION

To Dr. Omar Lopez an intuitive, multi-dimensional talent.

CHAPTER ONE
ABOUT SHAMANISM

Shamanism or whatever name it has been called is probably the oldest healing practice known to the human race. Archaeological evidence demonstrates shamanism is at least 40,000 years old. And even here, there is some debate. Some experts in the field of antiquity believe shamanic practices go back at least 100,000 years. Whatever its date, it has been around a long time. At outset, I want to point out that the words shamanism and shaman do not come from Native Americans. Each tribe has its own words for healer and healing; for example, nepiteget (ne-pe-tiget) in MiqMaq means healer. Nor do the original inhabitants of South America or Africa call their healers, shamans. So, then, where does the word shaman come from?

The word shaman is pronounced either as SHAY-man or SHA-man and like the time frame suggested for the existence of shamanism, it is subject to debate. Some scholars claim the words shaman and shamanism are so indiscriminately used; they no longer have meaning. They are like the word pretty. For example, who knows the meaning of pretty? It's a pretty day, or it's a pretty dress, or it's pretty nice, or it's pretty tough going, or it's pretty awful. Some claim a complete definition of shamanism is impossible.

The first reference to the word shaman comes to us in the late 1600s. Peter the Great of Russia had sent emissaries to China. Among those who went along were two Dutch diplomats. They, in writing back to Holland, used the word shaman and are credited for bringing the word into Western thought.

In 1875, the Encyclopedia Britannica published an article by A. H. Sayee in which he used the word shaman.

Scholarly opinion, however, indicates that the word shaman comes from Tungas and specifically from the Manchu-tangu dialect of Siberia. Yet, that has its challenge. Some ethnolinguists claim the word derives from the Chinese, scha-man and still others claim it's Pali, a Middle Indo-Aryan language native to the Indian subcontinent and others say it is from the Hindu Sanskrit.

Shaman and shamanism have now become popular terms in Western Culture and refer to a man or woman who fills several roles. Specifically, two aspects of shamanic healing have gained popularity: physical and psychological healing.

One of the major challenges of shamanism is the view held by some academics that it is a religion. The basis for this claim is the shaman's reliance upon the world of the spirits and she or he does so because they adhere to the belief that there is a direct connection between healing and the world of spirits. I suppose because a shaman calls upon the spirit world it would cause some to believe shamanism was a religion. However, unlike some of the world's religions, there is no indication that early shamanic practices included praying to various saints or deities besides the Directions. Additionally, there is no set dogma followed by all shamans nor is there a holy book, temples, mosques, cathedrals, or churches, nor were there schools to train young men or women to become healers. In Chapter Fourteen I'll discuss how one becomes a shaman, a healer.

Another claim is shamanism is a cult. It is not. Admittedly, some have linked themselves in a cult-like fashion to some of the fundamental healing practices of some Native Americans. The use of the sweat-lodge, going on a Vision Quest, and the use of hallucinogenics appear to be a drawing card for some and create the impression that shamanism is a cult. A few years ago, tragedy struck within a sweat lodge in Arizona. I will have more to say about Vision Quests and hallucinogens later in another chapter.

Unfortunately, some contemporary dictionaries define a shaman as one who uses magic to cure illnesses and control spiritual forces. A shaman does not use magic and despite some contemporary religious groups, shamanism is not evil. If one is a healer; one doesn't commit evil acts. The claim that a shaman controls spiritual forces is without merit.

Shamans may be divided into five types. As with some of the other aspects of shamanism, I have mentioned there are those who claim that distinguishing four types of shamans is splitting hairs. There is a simple reason for my making these distinctions, and that is to bring about an understanding of the various roles a shaman may be asked to fill. All traditional shamans have two things in common—they all journey or travel to other realms, and they all seek help and guidance from those that inhabit the spirit world.

The first type of shaman is the *healer* and as such will receive major emphasis throughout this course. The healer may travel to one or all three "realms": the Upper, Middle or Lower Realm to help heal a patient. Do not equate these realms with the religious concepts of Heaven, Purgatory, and Hell. Second, the healer will use various remedies based on natural plants. She or he will create salves, poultices, ointments, and teas from plants and berries. In days gone by, the healer would place certain plants around and directly on the patient but today because of potential allergic reactions I urge caution.

The second type of shaman is the *soul retriever*. The Soul Retriever travels to one of the three realms to gather up the soul or parts of a soul and return it to its human body. During this retrieval, the shaman may have a helper, a spirit guide, or a spirit animal. I will have more to say about this shamanic role in another module.

The third type of shaman is the *spiritual healer.* In today's world psychologists, psychiatrists, counselors, ministers, priests, rabbis, or imams deal with the emotional aspects of a person's life. The Spiritual Healer does much the same thing. He or she deals with the anger, frustration, jealousy, hate, prejudice, or self-defamation of a patient. Herbs, as well as sounds, become part of the treatment. The Spiritual Healer may place the patient in a hypnotic state, go into a trance to help the patient resolve her or his emotional-spiritual issues.

The fourth type of shaman is the *Messenger*. The Messenger brings information from the non-ordinary world to the real world. This information, in days gone by, may have dealt with immediate events, or those to come. Such things as the hunt, crop growth, a tribal move, or a tribal war may have been the focus of a message. The message may deal with all humanity. At any given time, shamans may fill all of these roles.

The fifth type of shaman is the Raconteur. At the outset, a Raconteur may not be a shaman. He or she is the keeper of the tribal wisdom, a provider of advice on issues of governance, marriage, child-bearing, and rearing. The raconteur, sometimes called the singer, is the storyteller. She or he recounts in word, song, or dance, the history of the tribe, its battles, tragedies, sacrifices, and sorrows. The story of the tribe's creation and its relationship to the divine is part of the raconteur's responsibilities. The raconteur is a historian who through the stories preserves the tribal history.

Whatever the role, be it, healer, or raconteur, the shaman is a highly respected, powerful, and often feared member of the tribal community. Many tribes kept their healer out of their village and forced them to live a considerable distance away from the village, often a solitary life. The shaman did come to the village for a special ceremony, to heal, or to find a mate.

What was the early shaman's *worldview*? Generally, when one thinks of a worldview, some grandiose scheme of things floods one's mind. Today, science is deeply involved in various theories of how the world came into existence. Probably the term worldview is likely too narrow a term to describe how a shaman views things. Perhaps the phrase *belief-system* is more appropriate. What then, do shamans believe? Universally, *first* among the major tenets is the lack of a need to confirm the world. For the shaman, what is—is. One cannot prove or disprove a perception. Perceptions are internalized and personal. Be mindful, however, one may change one's perception, and a shaman never hesitates to change hers or his if it is necessary.

Second, the shaman believes the Self and all else are connected, moving together in fluidity just as mind and matter are irrevocably intertwined. The fundamental basis for this tenet is the notion that all things contain a life force, a soul, or a spirit. This includes human beings, all animals, and plants. Mountains, rivers, streams, lakes, oceans, the wind, and the planetary system are considered to be part of all that is alive. This is important in that the shaman accepts all of these as potential helpers and as such he acknowledges all of them. Native American prayers amply demonstrate this. I will share part of one such prayer which shows the relationship to Earth. It is by KiiskeeN'tum (She Who Remembers) and is titled *Mother Earth.*

Mother Earth hear your child, as I sit here on your lap of grass, I listen to the echoes of your voice in my brother, the Wind, as he blows from all corners and directions.

The soft and gentle raindrops are the Tears you cry for your children.

Teach me the Lessons you offer: To nurture my children, as you nurture yours, To learn the Lessons of the Four Kingdoms, that make up this World of Physical Things, and To Learn to Walk the Path chosen so long ago.

The *third* aspect of the shamanic belief system is the concept that the individual is fundamentally responsible for her or his health. For the shaman, one's health is the creation of that individual. This is significant! The shaman functions primarily as a healer. The key here is the word creation. The shaman's job is to determine the cause for the malfunction of that creation. This holds unless an individual has had her or his soul or part of the soul stolen.

The *fourth* tenet is the shaman's view of reality. For the shaman, the reality is not just a physical representation. Both ordinary and non-ordinary realities exist in the shaman's view. The practiced shaman is comfortable in either reality. For the shaman, all realities are possible. Peggy Malnati in "The Shamanic View of the World (Walksoftly2's

Blog, 2011) writes "…. reality is perceived as being layered rather than flat and single-dimensional." She continues by saying, "Existence is not only perceived as being layered in parallel and overlapping horizontal dimensions but also it is layered vertically." Modern science supports this through the concept of parallel universes or multi-dimensionalism.

The fifth tenet of the shamanic world view involves the belief that the world, the universe, or the cosmos is a living, changing, evolving entity. It is alive and the shaman, in turn, flows with whatever those changes may be. This statement probably best represents the shamanic worldview: "I am that I am and the World is as I dream it."

The shaman's worldview is certainly substantiated by modern science. Today we know that all things are made of molecules that are in a state of constant movement creating the energy we call the life force. Thus, shamanically speaking, all things are indeed alive.

CHAPTER TWO
LINGA SHARIRA AND AURIC LAYERS

Early cultures have suggested human beings have a double; a doppelgänger, an alter ego or Linga Sharira[i]. Whatever name one chooses to give it, it's a Bioplasmic luminous glow that surrounds the physical body. All human beings including plants, animals, and all inurnment things are said to have these subtle bodies that give off a vibrational frequency of light. What then is a subtle body? To begin, it is quasi material, that is, it is neither just physical nor just spiritual. The Linga Sharira is viewed as the principal vehicle of Prâna, the life force of the body. It has a form of its own and is projected outside of the physical body and that is called an aura. Scientifically, is an Electromagnetic Field. This aura has designated colors with specific meanings.

Red indicates you are well-grounded, that is, stable, consistent.

Orange suggests you are thoughtful and considerate.

Yellow implies creativity and friendliness`

Green equals socially adept and nurturing

Blue indicates you are intuitive and spiritual

Indigo suggests you are curious and spiritually well connected

Violet implies wisdom and intellectualism.

In the interest of healing and the role of auras in the diagnostic processes, it is necessary to point out that there is, at this time, no significant scientific studies to prove even the existence of auras let alone any role they may or may not play in one's physical, mental and emotional health.

We do know the idea of subtle bodies dates at least back to the 2nd Century BCE and it has gradually evolved. In Hinduism, the Doctrine of Three Bodies states that the human being is composed of three shariras. These three bodies are the casual body, the subtle body, and the gross body.

This concept of subtle bodies in the Western world is referred to as bodies of light from the Greek philosopher, Plato. For him, 'astral' referred to the stars, that is "of the stars" and the astral plane was composed of the Seven Heavens from the classical concept of planets. Thus, this Bioplasmic luminous glow was divided into seven layers. These layers create an auric body or auras which extend out from the physical body for about three feet. The purpose of this auric body is to protect your physical body by keeping away negative vibrations, which could have the propensity to do you harm. For the shaman, they are a way of determining a client's physical, mental, and emotional states. The seven layers are:

1. Etheric is closest to the physical body. Existing anywhere from 2 to 4 inches away from the physical body and is generally the layer the

healer sees during a treatment session. Its color is light grey-violet or bluish grey and it is the easiest to see with the naked eye. It is connected to the Root Chakra and pulsates at 20 cycles per minute. The shaman will read that vibration and it is low there is a strong indication that the client's immune system is compromised.

2. Emotional layer sits just outside the physical body and extends out 1 to 3 inches. Connected to the Sacral Chakra that holds all of one's feelings. Generally, all colors of the rainbow may be represented, but if one is under emotional stress the colors will be muddy looking. The state of the other chakras can be determined from this layer.

3. Mental exists directly outside the emotional body and extends 3 to 8 inches from the physical body. It is the area of thoughts or cognition and it is a bright yellow. Connected to the Solar Plexus it radiates the strongest around the upper torso, specifically the head and shoulders. Its yellow color is strongest in those who are creatively active or in those who have an over-active mind-a mind filled with endless chatter.

4. Astral Layer extends about a foot out from the physical body. It is the bridge that connects us to our astral cords, that is, the connection between the lower and higher vibrations of the physical plane and that of the Spiritual plane. It is connected to the Heart Chakra. Its pink or rosy color is strongest in

loving relationships and is weakest during conflicts with loved ones. Since many physical, as well as emotional issues, are indicated at this layer, it is here that the shaman will spend some time providing treatment.

5. Etheric Template Layer extends about 24 inches out from the body. If you know what the negative of a photograph is you have a good image of his layer. Another way of looking at the Etheric Template Layer is to look at it as the blueprint of the body that exists on the physical plane. Your identity, personality, and bodily energy are included here. It is connected to the Throat Chakra and varies in color.

6. Celestial Layer is connected to the Third Eye Chakra and has a very strong and powerful vibration most likely because it connects to the Divine. It is the place where unconditional love is. It glows in a Pearly white color. At its strongest, an individual may be able to communicate with the Spirit World.

7. Ketheric Template or Spiritual Layer exists 2 to 3 feet from the physical body. It is the feeling of being one with the Universe and projects all the information about your soul and previous lifetimes. Connected to the Crown Chakra, it vibrates at the highest vibrancy which is reflected in its bright gold color. At its strongest, it can help increase one's psychic abilities.

If it is determined that there is significant entanglement within the layers the shaman will work to change the vibration pattern of the individual. A sweep of the client with a pendulum or dowsing rod will reveal improvement or lack of improvement after treatment.

An issue for the shaman is that these layers may each vary in their size and overall depth both of which depend on the physical size of the client and the place they are in their lives; career-wise, socially, and age. As a consequence of this variance in the layers, the shaman cannot give a blanket all-in-one healing treatment. Each layer must be treated separately and this may deplete the shaman's energy flow.

In other cultures, the Ancient Egyptians, for example, believed the human soul had three parts: the Ka, Ba, and Sa. The Ka is comparable to one's double. It may be the self-image you encounter while on a shamanic journey or an astral projection. If you do sense the Ka welcome it and ask that it reveal its purpose for its visit.

CHAPTER THREE
ASTRAL PROJECTION

Astral Projection is a term used to describe a deliberate out-of-body experience. The underlying assumption is that a subtle body exists and further, that this subtle body functions separately from the physical body. It means your consciousness leaves your physical body. That is, your Ka leaves your body to travel. Therefore, you can travel to different places realms, and or dimensions. The basic idea of such travel is not new. It is ancient. Some writers quote Paul's Second Epistle to the Corinthians as a reference to the astral planes: "I know a man in Christ who fourteen years ago was caught up to the third heavens." (2 Corinthians 12-2)

Astral Projection is generally not drug-induced as in "tripping." However, Psychologists Todd Girard of Ryerson University (Toronto) found that an anesthetic called Ketamine did create out-of-body illusions.[ii] Generally, the sound is used to create a hypnotic state. There is any number of CDs, videos, and Mp3 files available that are specifically designed for Astral Projection. There are at least five attributes to Astral Projection:

1. You are awake
2. You seem to step outside of your body
3. You are very aware of your physical being

4. You can see your physical body; not just an outline, but real details such as hair, eyes, mouth, body shape, etc.

5. Your Astral Projection begins from wherever your physical body is located.

6. You will have several reactions ranging from "Oh, my god" to "You've got to be kidding."

I will share two experiences I had with Astral Projection. I used an audiotape. I was growing a beard and had had it for a couple of months. I found myself standing and looking into our living room. I was reclining on a lounge. I heard myself say, "Now that's ugly." The tape ended. I immediately shaved off my beard. It was ugly! The second experience is completely different and I have no earthly explanation for it.

I began my session using the Astral Tape. I began to think nothing was going to occur. As the soundtrack was nearing its end and was in the process of bringing me back a handsome young man appeared. He had blond hair and brown eyes and a radiant smile. His lean muscular body suggested he was used to hard labor. Two days later the front doorbell clanged. I opened the door and there stood that same young man. I had ordered a cord of wood for the fireplace. He was delivering the wood.

From my perspective and experience, Shamanic Journeying's details are more readily remembered and recognized; whereas, they are not in Astral Projection. And there is a reason for that. First, and foremost, you are taking the Shamanic Journey to get an answer to a specific question. Remembering detailed information gained during a shamanic journey is important. As a healer, that information may help deal with a client's issues. After all, the purpose of the Journey is to gain useful information. Unlike Astral Projection, Shamanic Journeying is never for entertainment. It is never a parlor game.

Albert Fernando, author of *Oneironaut (O-Neiro-naut)* says, "Shamans can travel in their minds without leaving their physical bodies." (Answered, November 12, 2018). Whereas, Astral Projection generally requires sound; however, if you do not have sound tapes, CDs, etc. available the following exercise should work for you.

Chamomile Astral Projection
A cautionary note: Do not do this and drive an automobile or use heavy equipment. The purpose here is to put you in a quasi-state of sleep. For this exercise, you will need a notepad, pen or pencil, Chamomile Essential Oil, Chamomile Tea, a cup, hot water.

1. Make a cup of Chamomile Tea. You may use a tea bag or loose tea. Make sure your cup is warm before adding the hot water and tea. Let it steep for five minutes.

2. Slowly drink the tea.

3. Sit in a comfortable chair or lie on a couch or bed. Make sure your clothes are not too tight, Remove your shoes and socks.

4. Place one drop of Chamomile Essential Oil on the bottom of each foot, two drops on a wrist, and gently rub it in for two seconds. Place one drop behind each ear.

5. Close your eyes and let whatever thoughts you have float by without developing them.

6. Do pay attention to what you see, to where you are, and what time of day it is: morning, afternoon, evening, or night. If you see someone acknowledge them. If they want to show you something, allow it unless you feel uncomfortable. You may experience a past life situation since you are in a different geography or even in another dimension.

7. When you wake up, jot down anything you remember: sights, sounds, feelings, and or the suggested answer to your question.

CHAPTER FOUR
VIBRATION

The late Michael Harner is credited with the popularization of the word "Journeying". Harmer's book, *The Way of the Shaman* did much to bring shamanic healing techniques to the modern world. I like his use of the word Journeying because the traditional word 'trance' suggests something negative. Maybe spooky is a better word; whereas, journeying does not.

Not all indigenous people used hallucinogens to Journey. Sound has been and is used for that purpose. Sound, however, has another and certainly a more important role to play in the healing processes. Sound involves vibration. Vibration creates energy and your energy introduces you before you say a single word. Additionally, before I get into the details of sound and vibration, it's our vibration, not our appearance through which we recognize one another's souls.

Shaman of old did not know all the technical science behind vibrational healing as do modern shaman and modern medicine. For the early shaman, such knowledge was innate.

The Law of Vibration states that everything that exists in our universe, whether seen or unseen, broken down into and analyzed in its purest and most basic form, consists of pure energy which resonates and exists as a vibratory frequency or pattern. (Quora.com) Think about this for a moment: Nothing ever really rests including you.

Physical, mental, and emotional issues arise when the vibrational pattern gets out of sync. Each individual's vibration pattern is different but to be healthy that vibration needs to be aligned with that of the Earth, of the Cosmos itself. Further, it is quite normal for vibrations to function at high and low frequencies within you as well as everything around you. When dealing with energy, remember like-energy attracts like-energy; that is, if you exude positive energy, positive energy will be returned to you. If, on the other hand, it is negative energy then that is what you will have returned to you.

Accepting the notion that all things vibrate, living as well as non-living things, then it becomes reasonable that early shamans used to sound. The frequency of vibration impacts everything. Masuro Emoto, *The Hidden Messages in Water*, amply demonstrated the importance of the spoken word. Big deal, you say. Remember, the human body is composed of nearly 70% water. The shaman's chant is a significant tool in bringing about healing in a client. The use of Om is a good example. Try repeating that for a couple of minutes and see how much better you feel.

Science informs us that the unit of measurement for vibration is Hertz[iii]. A hertz is one cycle per minute. In the United States, our home electricity is 60 hertz. That means the electrical current changes direction 120 times or 60 cycles per second. Human hearing ranges from 20 to

20,000Hz. Further, our hearing is most sensitive in the 2000 - 5000 Hz frequency range. Castleton Tower in Utah vibrates at 1.0hz.

The human heart beats 1.75hz and the earth at 7.85hz. All things vibrate. Some are promoting the idea that consciousness itself, is vibration. Tam Hunt in "Resonance Theory-Could Consciousness all come down to the way things Vibrate?' (SciTech Daily Oct 14, 2021) states ". . . resonance-another word for synchronized vibrations-is at the heart of not only human consciousness but also animal consciousness and of physical reality." If that doesn't sound off a bit it should. Does vibration change physical reality? The shaman counts on it as a vehicle for journeying to other realms.

When our body's cells which normally vibrate between a 62-70hz drop in vibration the cells are said to be sick or damaged; they no longer replicate normally. With the correct application of sound, these cells can be re-activated, that is, energized. Healing takes place. The shaman uses various tools to reactivate the client's cells such as drums, flutes, and rattles. Tibetan and crystal bowls are now added to healing sessions. Tools used in healing are discussed in Chapter Five.

Clients invariably want to know if they have a low or high vibration. Generally, high vibrations are associated with positive aspects of one's life. These positive vibrations include love, compassion, forgiveness, and a sense of personal peace. Qualities such as hatred, fear, greed, holding a grudge, low self-esteem, and depression are associated with low vibration. Physical illness falls within the low vibration category. I discuss ways of determining vibration levels in a client in Module Twelve.

The shaman during the initial client interview and body scan will note if signs are indicating low vibration. A cautionary note: You are not necessarily one hundred percent of either low or high, but somewhere in between. Here are 8 very general low vibration indicators.

1. You feel you are in a rut. It's that sameness that creates monotony and boredom.

2. You have a sense of being apathetic; that is, you have no empathy for others.

3. You are tired all the time.

4. It is difficult for you to be forgiving, especially of yourself.

5. You find it difficult to maintain lasting friendships; that is, you tend to be a loner.

6. You are self-defaming and not as an effort to be humorous.

7. You do not know what it is you want.

8. You feel others do not appreciate what you do.

What then, are the indicators that you have high vibration? As with the low vibration, you are seldom 100% high vibrations, but somewhere in between.

1. You are very aware of what you say, of what you feel, and the impact this has on others.

2. You express empathy toward others including animals and the environment.

3. You have a sense of connection to that which is otherworldly.

4. You nurture others as well as yourself.

5. Others find you easy to talk to because you listen.

6. You are open to many different beliefs and cultures.

7. You feel you have found your 'calling' in life.

8. You are highly intuitive.

The easiest way to decide the level of your vibration, that is whether it is low or high, is to simply pay close attention to how you feel especially when you get up in the morning.

If a client has a low vibration, I often suggest he or she do the following before having a shamanic healing session. I also may suggest these as an after-treatment follow-up. Please keep in mind, these are suggestions, and neither I nor any other qualified healer will say these are a cure.

1. Take stock of your thoughts. Are they negative? Do you dwell on an unpleasant experience? If so, name the thought or experience and then say, "I don't need you. Go!" Say that with a strong feeling.

2. Take a good look at your surroundings. Focus on something you think is beautiful or something that makes you feel warm and comfortable.

3. Cut back on the sugars. Add some more protein to your diet. Eliminate TV snack foods.

4. Increase your intake of water. My yoga teacher is always admonishing me to drink more water. Doing so gets rid of the toxins that slow your natural vibrations.

5. Physically move about. Go for a walk; do yoga or qi gong for example.

6. Do deep breathing exercises for ten minutes. Use Prana Breathing or Ujjayi Breathing techniques, or any other deep breathing technique that you prefer.

7. Listen to solfeggio recordings. Several excellent Mp3 files are available on the Internet that can be downloaded for free.

8. Express your gratitude to yourself and the universe.

It is known that sound has different frequencies. We emit our sound vibrations. The secret to healing with sound is matching frequencies. The shaman uses sound that she or he creates by using rattles, flutes, cymbals, and or drums. The shaman moves around the client's body while creating sounds.

The *Mindvalley* blog, dated January 10, 2019, lists several ailments in which sound improves the condition: autism, depression, and anxiety disorder for example. Additionally, the article lists several areas positively affected by sound healing. Clarity, improved memory, and heightened awareness are examples. Specific hertz is used to create various states of perception. Faena Aleph in *Eight healing Techniques with Sound*[iv] lists four areas in which specific hertz are used. For example, concentration is improved at the 12-40 Hz level.

Shamans have used sound to help their clients heal from time immemorial. Modern research has slowly verified much of what is done in sound healing.

If you feel you are experiencing low vibration, on a sheet of paper write down what you feel may be causing that low vibration. Once you have your list (Your list may be just one item), tear it up, and in a safe place, burn it. Then say, out loud or to yourself, "I am free!"

CHAPTER FIVE
ELEVEN SHAMANIC TOOLS

Healing is most certainly one of the most important roles a shaman plays. Some would say, it is the most important. And not unlike, the doctors of today, the shaman had the tools of the day available to her or him. But before I get into the actual tools a shaman uses to heal and to connect to the spirit world, there is an aspect of the shamanic worldview that requires an early-on explanation—and that is the shamanic relationship to the Columna Cerulli (co lum nà Ce ruli).

The Columna Cerulli is often called the Tree of Life or The Tree of Knowledge as it is found in Judaism and Christianity. Sometimes it is also called the Central Axis of the Cosmos. It means the center of that which is and as such it holds importance in many ancient cultures and most likely has existed since humankind became acculturated.

The earliest known record of the Columna Cerului comes to us from the Ancient Egyptian story of Osiris. However, some scholars claim the idea more likely is from the works of Hermes Trismegistus (Tris-meg-is-tus) which is collectively known as the *Hermetica*. As a symbol, it is embedded in mythology, religion, and science. In addition to Egypt, the literature of Assyria and China references such a concept. Besides Judaism and Christianity, it appears in Bahà, Hinduism, and

Mormonism. Whatever, the origin, it references the world center and as such, is viewed as a universal concept. It is represented in the first shamanic tool.

<u>The staff is the first tool</u> of the shaman. It is

sometimes called the *talking stick*. Its function varies depending upon the need perceived by the shaman. Whatever, its function, the talking stick is viewed as a power tool. It represents Columna Cerulli and is held in high regard. It is treated with respect and treated with care.

The Columna Cerului presents a paradox for the shaman. The reason such a paradox exists in that the shaman believes the center of the world is everywhere. In an altered state of consciousness, the shaman physically remains firmly planted in the ordinary world. When in the trance state, the Columna Cerului becomes the spot on which the shaman stands or sits. It becomes the center of the universe.

Because the talking stick is such a powerful tool it is considered to be *Amitai*, that which is alive. Physically, the staff is made of maple or oak and may have a variety of decorations such as a carved totem, a rawhide strung with beads, quills, sacred animal bones, feathers, and in some cases the staff may have dried gourds attached. These, when the talking stick is shaken, become an elongated rattle.

It is believed the staff makes it possible to increase spiritual power for the shaman. As such, the staff contains a master spirit. This makes the talking stick a connection to the three realms and allows the shaman access to those areas. The shaman takes the talking stick and pounds the ground or the floor if inside. It's like knocking on a door. The shaman also uses it to call her or his spiritual helper.

There are many written examples of the staff as a power tool. Two come to mind: Moses of the Old Testament, and of course, King Arthur and the marvelous Merlin. By hitting the floor with the staff, the modern shaman is changing the vibrational pattern of the client as well as the physical setting where the healing session is taking place.

Smudging is the second tool and it involves the burning of several herbs in a small dish or a seashell. I use a combination of white sage, cedar, and Palo Santo. I use these crushed rather than ground. I place a small amount on a dish, light it, and fan it with a turkey feather around my client. The reason for doing this is to clear any negative energy that the client may have. However, if I am cleansing a room or a house, I use a white sage bundle to clean out negative energy. Sometimes, however, it may be used to remove unwanted spirits from a dwelling.

Several years ago, I was asked to cleanse a beautiful mansion that had been the scene of a murder. I used White sage from California. Whatever the spirit dwelled there, left.

When lit, the sage becomes a burning ember and gives off a pleasant aroma. There are seven varieties of sage that are good for smudging: Garden, Pineapple, Russian, Purple, Golden, Berggareten, and White Mountain.

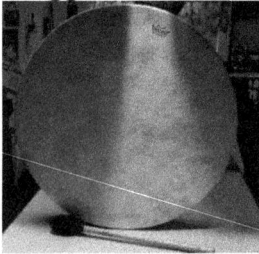

The drum is the third tool and the most recognizable tool in the shaman's repertoire is the drum and it holds a significant place among the shaman's tools. And like, modern drums, the shamanic drum comes in various sizes from handheld to those that sit on the floor. My focus is on handheld drums. Deer, Elk, or Buffalo skins are used in drum construction. My drum (pictured), however, is of man-made materials and because it is, it is not subject to weather conditions as are those made from animal skins. It's a personal preference.

By using the drum, the shaman attempts to reintroduce harmony between the client's mind, body, and soul. The drum changes the vibrational flow of the client. More will be said about vibration in another class.) The drum is also used to help the shaman go into a trance to travel to another realm. It helps the shaman to move from ordinary reality to non-ordinary reality. In the culture of the Australian, this state is known as Dreamtime.

Today, this shift is referred to as the shamanic journey. More will be said about journeying in another class and the travel to other realms.

The implied therapeutic value of drumming is enjoying a resurgence. Classes in drum making, playing drums, and drumming circles are popping up throughout the country. Parlayed as being helpful, drumming's value now includes the reduction of stress, lower blood pressure, a reduction of muscular aches and pains, as well as some psychological issues.

Sometimes, the shaman will have someone else do the drumming. In addition to helping the shaman to go into a hypnotic state, it allows the shaman to use another tool. In this instance, that tool is the dance. Even though the dance is not a physical object per se, it is nonetheless an important tool in bringing about a positive change in the vibrational flow of a client. The shaman will have rattles attached to each ankle and have a rattle in his hand to harmonize with the steady monotonous beat of the drum. The shaman dances around the client. The drumming and the rattles bring the shaman's body rhythm and physical resonance into sync with the natural world and by that, I mean the actual physical rhythmic beat of the Earth. The Earth's vibration is about 7.83 Hz.

Check out "The Earth Seen from ISS" at the following link:

https://www.youtube.com/watch?v=oGYv3sCuxVQ)[v]

A fourth tool is the shaman's medicine bags. There are two general types of medicine bags used by practicing shamans. Both are highly personal and often reflect the shaman's knowledge and skills. Modern versions might still be a pouch and something similar to a gym bag.

The first bag is a small leather pouch attached to a rawhide string and worn around the neck. It could be worn around the hip. If it is a male shaman there most likely will be very little decoration or none. Decorations may be in the form of beads, an abstract design, and a fringe along the bottom. This bag is considered a power bag, that is, it is a source of energy and power for the shaman. The bag may contain some or all of the following items: a bear claw, earth-warmed small stones, bones of a spirit animal, a feather, a small stick of sage, or any other thing the shaman values. This pouch is sacrosanct. (Upload photo of pouch)

The second bag is also made of leather and may or may not be decorated. Sometimes, there is a sacred symbol created with vegetable dyes. If there are any symbols, they generally are representative of power animals such as a bear. The bag may contain a ceremonial mask, rattles, various herbs, other medicinal plants, totems, tobacco, and ground cornmeal. It might be about the size of a World War

II military duffel bag. The bag might also contain natural substances to cause a flame or a flare-up, or to create large amounts of smoke to give the shaman a chance to change masks. A small hand drum may be included.

Rattles, the fifth tool, are often called Hands of the Spirit, and as the drum, help in altering the shaman's state of consciousness. Frequently, they are the primary means of Spirit World communication. And like the drum, they are used to help induce an altered state of consciousness; thus, opening the doorway for journeying. Rattles are used to change the client's vibration patterns and to relieve energy blockages.

Rattles may be made of clamshells, turtle shells, pine cones, horse chestnuts that function as bells. Generally, the rattles are made of dried gourds. Sometimes, additional small seeds or stones are inserted into the gourd to create more sound. For ease of use, a wooden stick may be inserted as a handle. Depending on the skill of the maker, some rattles may take the shape of animals, abstract, but recognizable. The one pictured was made for me and is constructed of animal skin, seeds, feathers, and wood. (Upload photo)

The sixth tool is the flute. Not being a flute player, I use a very small flute to make a sound. I repeat that sound over and over. Again, the purpose here is to change the vibrational pattern of the

41

client. (Upload photo of flute) Here's one example of the use of a flute- Alexandro Querevalu playing the flute.

https://www.youtube.com/watch?v=Dgo1vqQf WN8.

Early shamans dressed in animal skins, had masks, and bird feathers

The seventh tool is the mask, which, throughout history, has had many roles: for power, to hide identity, and to connect with the Spirit World. Often, the shaman's mask was used to identify with a spirit animal. When dressed in full regalia, the mask added the necessary touch to hold the client in awe and suggestive of special power. The mask also helped to hide the real identity of the shaman as he or she traveled in the spirit world, particularly if evil spirits were lurking about. The mask in the photo was a gift and is not something I use.

An eighth tool is an Extractor. I have no idea as to how long-ago Crystal Extractors were used. But because it is one of my favorite healing tools, I am including it here. Sometimes the Extractor is referred to as a Generator. Generally, the Extractors are diamond-shaped. However, the Extractor I use has four prongs of

Obsidian encased in silver and attached to a pyramid-shaped clear Quartz crystal.

An Extractor may be used to move or remove energy, to amply energy to heal, and to relieve pain. I use it to relieve physical pain as well as emotional pain. If, for example, my client has thumb issues, I place the flat bottom of the Quartz Pyramid directly on the fatty part of the thumb area and have the client hold it there for a good two minutes. After that, I turn the Extractor so that the point of the Quartz Pyramid is gently pressed into the painful area. Again, I have the client hold it there for two minutes. The flat part removes the pain while the pointed part of the Obsidian Extractor brings in healing energy.

If the client is experiencing an emotional issue, I have them on the massage table, on their back, and I place the Obsidian Extractor at the center of the forehead, flat side down. The Extractor stays in place for five minutes. Instead of turning the Extractor over so the point rests on the forehead, I remove it and replace it with an Amethyst crystal.

A ninth tool is Shamanic Breathing. Shamanic Breathing provides a two-prong use: First, it is an excellent tool for creating balance and harmony in both the physical and emotional body. Second, it can replace the use of the drum or other sounds to journey.

In today's world, it is common for us to become irritated, frustrated, and angry. We tend to hold on to taught belief systems that place us in conflict with ourselves as well as with those around us. The workplace, home, spouses, children, and or lovers tend to wear on our nerves. Shamanic Breathing goes a long way in reducing that stress; it helps us get past it to a calmer and healthier life.

Walid Aboulnaga[vi] lists the following reasons why people seek Shamanic Breathing Techniques:

1. Searching for Healing and Spiritual Change
2. Seeking Transformation in their lives
3. Wanting to Expand Consciousness
4. Searching for Clarity, Vision, and Guidance

As with other suggestions in this book, there is a cautionary note: Persons who have any of the following conditions should not try Shamanic Breathing: heart issues, high blood pressure, eye issues, epilepsy, or recent surgery. Women who are pregnant should avoid Shamanic Breathing. With that said, what are the necessary preparations to engage Shamanic Breathing?

1. Avoid alcohol for 24 hours before doing Shamanic Breathing
2. Have nothing to eat at least two full hours before beginning your breathing session
3. Have a very specific and conscious intention
4. Do a Palo Santo, white sage, or cedar smudge before you start.

Here are the four steps to do Shamanic Breathing:

1. Breathe in. Count to four slowly
2. Hold your breath for 4 seconds

3. Slowly exhale through your open mouth for 4 seconds

4. Repeat the previous 3 steps until you sense a return of balance and harmony.

Using Shamanic Breathing to Journey is just as effective as the use of sounds or hallucinogens. If you have heart issues, high blood pressure, eye issues, epilepsy, or have had recent surgery **do not do** this activity. If you are pregnant, **do not do** this activity. Follow the steps previously outlined. Be sure you have a specific reason for journeying. For example: What happened to my friend Joey? Increase the time for the breathwork to fifteen to twenty minutes. At the end of that time, close your eyes and breath normally. Think of your question. You may go to sleep. That's fine. Allow yourself to float out. Be prepared to greet whomever you meet.

A tenth tool is Shamanic Meditation and it is to be used to help those who suffer hypertension, anxiety, chakra imbalance, and low energy flow. To help ensure that this tool works there are a few things that you should do before attempting it. No alcohol or drugs at least 24 hours before the Shamanic Meditation. It is also a good idea not to have eaten a heavy meal, loaded up on sweets and coffee.

Shamanic Meditation involves visualizing, that is, a mental image is required to aid concentration. Any peaceful image is acceptable. Some individuals may find the repetition of a short mantra works.

Follow the procedures for Shamanic Breathing.

Shamanic Meditation benefits your energy flow thus improving the function of your vital organs. A benefit that is sometimes overlooked is the cleansing of the whole-body system that takes place. Anxiety, depression, and anger will gradually lessen. Above all, do not be judgmental. Remember, practice makes perfect.

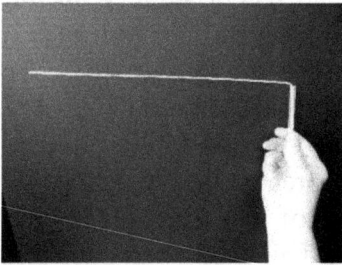

The eleventh tool is the **Dowsing Rod.** I do not claim that the Dowsing Rod was a tool used by ancient healers. It has long been used to find water and in more modern times, to locate underground power lines. I use a metal dowsing rod made from a coat hanger. I cut the bottom wire, and bend one end so the letter L is formed. On the short end, I place a piece of clear plastic straw. It is this I hold between my thumb and first finger. I do this so the rod moves freely and to demonstrate I am not moving it. I walk around a client to determine her or his energy flow. Before I do that, I have the client hold the dowsing rod so they can see for themselves that the rod moves freely in the plastic straw. When the rod stops moving that is an indication of a possible energy block and it is there that I begin the healing treatment.

One further use of the dowsing rod is the determination of spirit energy in a room. If you want to check for a possible spirit, hold the rod in your dominant hand and walk around the room. Electrical outlets, equipment, computers, and TV will have an effect. Spirits will not be hiding in those areas. Look in closets or dark corners of a room. Most spirits are not bad; a few may be jokesters.

CHAPTER SIX
PLANT MEDICINE AND ITS USE

Between 1951 and 1960, anthropologist Ralph Solecki of Columbia University and his team working in the Shanidar Cave in Iraq discovered 10 mummified bodies that have now been dated to be 70,000 years old. The tenth body contained 8 medicinal plants strongly suggesting the man was a healer. The other bodies did not have these plants. The plants were Yarrow, Cornflower, Batchelor's Button, St. Barnaby's Thistle, Ragwort, Marshmallow, Grape Hyacinth, and Hollyhock.

Today, we know that Yarrow, for example, was used for fevers, diarrhea, and other gastrointestinal issues. Ragwort is classified as an herb and its leaves are used to create herbal medicine. There is considerable concern over the use of Ragwort because it contains chemicals that may block blood flow. Again, do not use plant medicines without checking with your medical doctor.

The first physical evidence of the use of plants for healing purposes came with the discovery of frozen a male corpse that was 5,300-year-old. He is now called the Iceman or Otzi. His remains were found in the Italian Alps in 1991. He is significant because he had a pouch with two chunks of mushrooms, Piptoporus betulinus whose common name is birch bracket. This mushroom was used to fight an intestinal parasite. A detailed autopsy showed Otzi had an intestinal parasite. This aspect of the discovery of the Ice Man provides the oldest evidence of early man practicing medicine.

For centuries the Chinese, as well as the Indians (Ayurveda), have treated the ills from a holistic point of view. Traditional shamanic treatment also included the physical as well as the psychological sphere of the human condition. Native American healers, as well as healers in other cultures, include not only the body, and mind but added spirit.

During the last century, particularly during the 1970s, we saw a trend in then-contemporary medicine that has continued forward and that trend is a holistic approach to patient treatment. That idea was not new; however, in 1926, Jan C. Smuts re-introduced that idea. He called it Holism. Holism is the theory that the parts of a whole are in an intimate interconnection. Medically this means the treatment of the "whole" person, that is, the physical, emotional, and environmental factors that impact an individual and not just the disease symptoms.

The shamanic approach to healing is the belief that the health of the individual is inextricably connected to one's surroundings. Consequently, the shaman works to promote harmony between the body, mind, and spirit as well as harmony with the patient's community, environment, and Spirit World.

There are four primary healing practices common to all shamans. These practices include the use of herbs for purging, and or extraction, ceremonies of purification, and contacting the Spirit World. Because of the strong belief that all things in nature are connected and that there is a corresponding relationship to the Spirit World, the shaman (including modern shaman) accepts the notion Spirits can help maintain, promote, and return one to good health.

As part of the connection to Nature, the shaman relies on a wide variety of herbs and other medicinal plants or what is often referred to as Plant Medicine. So, what is an herb?

An herb is the green, leafy part of the plant; whereas, a spice is made from the roots of the plant. Shown is the herb, Basil[vii]. Herbs are used as food flavorings but not all medicinal plants are edible. For our purpose, herbs used for medicine have all parts of the plant used unless it is poisonous.

A partial list of potentially harmful herbs if ingested includes Arnica, Belladonna, Bittersweet, Jimsonweed, Foxglove, and Mayapple. The *Physician's Desk Reference for Herbal Medicine* is an excellent source of information.

93% of all plants are not edible but with that being said, early shamans still knew over 2,000 medicinal plants. Seventy-five percent of the world's population continues to rely primarily upon traditional healing practices, particularly the use of herbs. Approximately 70,000 species of plants have been screened for their potential utility for medicine. According to the U.S. Forest Service, "a full 40 of the drugs behind the pharmacists' counter in the Western world are derived from plants." At least 118 prescriptions are based on natural sources: 74 percent come from plants, 18 percent from fungi, 5 percent from bacteria, and 3 percent from vertebrate species such as snakes or frogs (Ecology Society of America).

What do you do if you want to use herbs in your healing? Today, there are herbalists. An herbalist might be a naturopath, a holistic medical doctor, or an herbal pharmacist. Check to see if there are courses offered locally. David Crow offers excellent courses in herbs and herbal remedies. He can be contacted at https://www.floracopeia.com.

To locate qualified herbalists, check The American Herbalist Guild at http://www.americanherbalistsguild.com/

Herbs are made into teas, poultices, salves, pastes, rubs, and soups. They are used for many physical, mental, and emotional issues including help with lucid dreaming, journeying, and manifesting. I have selected a few of the more interesting and useful herbs to talk about.

Disclaimer: First, I am not prescribing the use of these herbs. Second, I firmly believe that before you use any supportive medicines you should consult with your medical physician. Third, these are suggestions and that does not imply that I am urging their use. Admittedly, I do use them in my healing practice and only with very specific approval from my clients.

Mugwort has a variety of other names including Felon Weed, Sailor's Tobacco, and Naughty Man. The Mugwort leaves act as a diuretic. It helps regulate menopausal symptoms, and functions as a mild sedative. It may be used for colds and fever. A bath with Mugwort provides relief for rheumatism. It is claimed that a small pillow used to sleep on, filled with Mugwort will produce prophetic dreams. Finally, a Mugwort smudge or tea acts as a cleansing tool. Old negative energies are removed.If a client is dealing with negative energies and that includes negative thought patterns the shaman may use a smudge made of Mugwort. Using a fan, the smoke from the burning Mugwort is wafted over the body of the client. After the session, Mugwort tea is offered. It has been reported that there are 11.6 billion microplastic particles in just one teabag, therefore, those who may be concerned about the consumption of microplastic particles from tea bags, use loose tea.

Chamomile is also called Mayhem, Ground Apple, and Whig Plant. The word *chamomile* is the Greek word for *Earth Apple* and that makes sense because Chamomile has an apple smell about it. Chamomile is used as a sedative and when applied externally it helps heal burns. In a piece of cheesecloth add Chamomile leaves soaked in warm water and place it over the eyes for a refreshing and restful few minutes. Made into an ointment Chamomile is used for eczema. Inhaling its steam is good for phlegm. Cautionary note: Some people may have an allergic reaction to Chamomile. Be sure you test before using Chamomile. Made for a spray, it's good for tree diseases and helps plants to grow. There are two kinds of Chamomile: Roman and German.

Roman Chamomile flowers are used to make medicines and food flavoring. It helps with various digestive issues such as an upset stomach, flatulence, and nausea. It's a good germ killer and can be applied to the skin. Roman Chamomile is said to contain an anti-cancer fighting chemical and may be of help in the battle with diabetes. As with other herbs, more study is needed regarding Chamomile's effect on cancer and diabetes.

German Chamomile can be taken by mouth for gas, travel sickness, hay fever, diarrhea, and attention deficit-hyperactivity disorder (ADHD). Other uses include breast soreness, hemorrhoids, skin irritation caused by radiation and it can be inhaled as an aid in treatment for respiratory tract irritations.

A former client, a nurse who helps in the delivery of babies, had experienced an especially difficult time with a patient resulting in the loss of the baby. After a one-and-a-half-hour Shamanic Healing, I suggested she drink a cup of Chamomile tea each evening about an hour before retiring. In this way, she was able to avoid using drugs that induce sleep and antidepressants and their negativity. Three days later, I talked with her and she was at peace and sleeping at night. After a healing session, I always check back with the client to see how they are doing.

Watercress, also known as Scurvy Grass, earned an excellent reputation as a healing herb early on. There is a record of its use in 400 BC. At that time, Hippocrates (from whom the medical profession gets its professional oath) had made certain a supply of Watercress was readily available.

Modern science identifies at least 15 essential vitamins and minerals contained in Watercress; for example, it contains more iron than spinach, more calcium than milk, and more vitamin C than oranges do. It's loaded with Vitamin K which strengthens bones and helps limit neuronal damage in the brain. And finally, Vitamin A is responsible for a healthy immune system and pigments in the retina of the eye. Manganese, B-carotene, B-6, B-complex, thiamin, pantothenic acid, riboflavin, zeaxanthin, and lutein and niacin complete the 15 essential vitamins and minerals.

Because watercress is high in antioxidants it has the potential to lower the risk of chronic diseases. It contains compounds that protect against cancer and promote heart health and boosts the immune system.

When infused, it makes a good tonic. Add apple, lemon, cucumber, and Watercress to boiling water. Add honey to make a cough syrup. Don't forget to use it in a sandwich instead of lettuce.

Cautionary note: If you are on a blood thinner do not eat Watercress. Do not eat watercress if you use Chlorzoxazone, Lithium, or Warfarin. Large amounts used over the long term can cause stomach and kidney problems. It is considered unsafe during pregnancy and breastfeeding.

An additional cautionary note is important: If you eat raw watercress make sure you have thoroughly washed it otherwise there may be harmful pathogens and toxins that can be ingested.

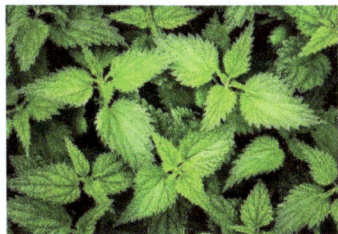

Nettles are sometimes called Nessels or Needles or Stinging Nettles. If not handled with care, Nettles can cause very unpleasant skin irritation. Unfortunately, I experienced a burning of my knees and legs after having trampled through a bunch of Nettles. When harvesting Nettles be sure to wear thick gloves. Pick the first two or three top pairs of leaves and carefully put them in a paper or plastic bag. Even though one generally picks Nettles in the spring, they can still be harvested in the fall. Avoid stalks and stems of the plant because they are generally tough. Not only do Nettles have medicinal uses they are edible.

Medicinally, Nettles are high in Vitamin C and Iron. Once cooked, they can be eaten as a spring tonic. Nettle juice can be used to treat certain skin conditions. It is known to help with anemia and diabetes. Nettle tea can be used for arthritis and Nettle compresses can be used to give relief to sore joints. Nettles, as a diuretic, is used for urinary tract infections, high blood pressure, congestive heart failure, premenstrual syndrome, benign prostate enlargement. Nettles taken in capsule form, provide relief for hay fever.

Cautionary note: First do not give Nettles to children two years old or under. Nettles are a diuretic and may deplete the body of necessary potassium and as such, it is not recommended to use Nettles as a means of weight loss.

Mushrooms should be considered even though they may not be technically classified as herbs. They are, nevertheless, an intricate part of the healing offered up by Mother Earth. Mushrooms have skyrocketed as aiding the control or cure for many diseases including MS, Parkinson's, and Cancer. Among the popular suggested mushrooms are Maitake, Turkey Tail, Reishi, and Lion's Mane. These now come in capsule, tincture, and powder form. All are good for the immune system.

Of the four, I will discuss Maitake Mushrooms as an example. The word Maitake is Japanese and it means "dancing mushroom." It is also called Hen-of-the-Woods, Ram's Head, or Sheep's Head. Because Maitake is an adaptogen, it is excellent as a body's assist in fighting any type of mental or physical difficulty. Generally viewed as medicinal the Maitake Mushroom can be used in recipes. It grows at the bottom of Oak trees, Elm and Maple Trees. Rich in antioxidants and amino acids the Maitake becomes excellent support for the immune system. There is an implication that the Maitake is effective in the treatment of cancer, side effects of chemotherapy, HIV/AIDS, chronic fatigue syndrome, high blood pressure, and cholesterol.

As with all supportive medicine, be sure to check with your medical doctor. The use of Maitake Mushrooms may have issues with pregnancy and breastfeeding, diabetes, blood pressure, and surgery.

There is a Mushroom Plant that is cultivated and contains many nutrients such as iron, beta-carotene, vitamins A, and C. It is a green leafy plant with blue-violet flowers. It is a nice substitute for those who do not like the texture of regular mushrooms but do enjoy the flavor.

Rosemary, one of my favorite herbs to use in my healing practice, is well known as a flavoring for foods. For hundreds of years, maybe even thousands, Rosemary has been used to strengthen memory. Burn it as incense to strengthen your memory. It stimulates the circulatory, digestive, and nervous systems. It is recommended as a treatment for headaches, indigestion, depression, and neuropathy. It helps relieve nasal and lung congestion as well as some allergies. As with some of the other prominent herbals, it is being researched as a cancer preventive.

A client comes to me complaining about low energy. I do an energy survey with my dowsing rod and if it indicates low energy, I place a white sock containing crushed Rosemary leaves on each foot. I then continue the healing session. Other times, I will place Rosemary leaves, in boiling water and have the client quietly inhale the steam for a stuffy nose or headache. More will be said about Rosemary as an essential oil.

Herbs are used for cleansing and supporting our respiratory system. Because our respiratory system never stops working it can be contaminated with pollutants and irritated. Herbs are helpful in that they may be used as an expectorant; used to soothe the nasal passages, and can fight the harmful organism that creates respiratory problems.

Eucalyptus is used to soothe a sore throat. Lungwort, which I use, helps clear congestion. Oregano, found in many foods, helps nasal passage airflow. Plantain Leaf helps to relieve a dry cough. Another herb I use is Elecampane. It helps smooth the tracheal muscles. And finally, Peppermint, a common food additive, is a good one to use as a therapeutic chest balm, rubbed on the abdomen for cramps, and across the forehead for headache.

CHAPTER SEVEN
ESSENTIAL OILS

Essential oils are also called volatile, ethereal, and aetherolea oils. Often an essential oil is referred to as the oil of-oregano or the oil of rosemary, for example. But what is an essential oil? It is a concentrated hydrophobic liquid. Generally, hydrophobic means to fear water, however, in chemistry, hydrophobic refers to the property of a substance to repel water. The remaining liquid contains aroma compounds from the plants.

How is this hydrophobic liquid extracted from plants? There are several ways by which the essence of plant oils is extracted. Among these are steam distillation, $Co2,$ absolutes, cold pressing, solvent extraction, maceration, enfleurage, and water distillation. The most common method of extraction is steam distillation. This involves the flow of steam into a chamber holding raw plant material. To give you an idea of the plant essence that is extracted you can try this on your own. Take a few leaves of fresh rosemary and place the leaves in a cup of boiling water. Let it cool down to room temperature and then remove the rosemary leaves. You will see a "slick" on top of the water. That's the essential oil, the essence of the plant.

The following figures give you an idea of the magnitude of the processes in creating essential oils. It takes 2,000 pounds of rose petals to make just 16 ounces of essential oil. It is said that it takes 20 to 25 roses to make one ounce of petals. It takes 50 pounds of Eucalyptus leaves to make an ounce of Eucalyptus oil, 220 pounds of Lavender flowers to produce one pound of essential oil, 500 pounds of Rosemary plants, and 1000 pounds of Jasmine flowers to produce one ounce of their essential oils. It's easy to see why essential oils are so expensive.

And that brings me to another issue. Unfortunately, not all essential oils are pure. Care and caution are the operative words here. Some oils are mostly jojoba, a wax ester, or some other carrier and may contain very little essential oil. A couple of years ago I visited a metaphysical shop and saw a small one-ounce bottle of Moldavite oil. An old saying, "A fool and his money are soon parted," applies here. It contained a small dark speck and cheap perfume. Be wary of food stores, drug stores, and novelty stores that sell "pure" essential oils. Make sure your source is a certified aromatherapist. Always ask them what their source is for their essential oils. The quality of soil makes a difference in the strength of the oil.

A cautionary note is necessary here. Do not apply 100% pure essential oil directly to your skin. Burns or some other skin irritation may result. Check with your doctor before using any essential oil. And this cautionary note brings me to the shamanic uses of essential oils.

Healers of old did not call the oils they used essential oils. A good guess is that they were not anywhere near what we now call essential oils. The shaman used the sap from various trees, crushed berries, soaked leaves, cooked roots of plants. Soups were made from plants, salves, poultices, and ointments were made from animal fat. Typically, the shaman uses oils for several different physical and emotional issues: for example, skin irritations, headaches, stomach upset, sore muscles, and a variety of diseases.

Essential oils may also be used for spiritual ceremonies and as an aid in journeying to the spirit world. Remember, before using any essential oil always test the oil or blend on a small area of your skin before using. If you have no issues with oil, then add two or three drops to a wrist and rub your writs together for a few seconds. It takes only 20 seconds for the essential oil to get into the bloodstream; 20 minutes for it to go through the whole body.

Even though today there is a good deal of emphasis on the healing qualities of essential oils on the physical level, their impact on the spiritual plane should not be minimized. Several essential oils have a propensity for enhancing the spiritual experience. And as with herbs and crystals, many essential oils can be and are used for many different things.

I will begin with some essential oils that help in the realm of spirituality. For those of you who have an interest in awakening spiritually, there are several essential oils you could consider. Three of my favorite oils that I use with my clients who are experiencing spirituality issues are *Cedarwood*, **Palo Santo**, and **Frankincense**.

Cedarwood Essential Oil I prefer comes from the Atlas Mountains of Algeria and Morocco. The word cedar is from *Cedrus*, from the Arabic word *Kedron* meaning power. And it is a powerful oil for grounding. I place two to three drops on a client's feet and gently rub it in when there is a good deal of tension present.

Cedarwood is known for its ability to cleanse spaces of negative energy. It does the same for individuals having spirituality issues. I recommend two cedarwood applications: first, spray the area with cedarwood hydrosol; second, place a small dish containing Cedarwood Essential oil on a nearby table   It helps heal the present. When I speak of spirituality issues, I am not talking about religions here but *prana. Prana is* that which makes one a human being.

Cedarwood has a calming effect when one is stressed and helps eliminate poor concentration. By the way, because of its woody smell, it is a popular fragrance with men. If there is general stress in the household, place 5 drops of Cedarwood Essential Oil in a diffuser.

Palo Santo is a tree that grows along the coast of South America and Mexico. The words mean "sacred wood" and sometimes it is referred to as "Holy Tree." Palo Santo is one of the outstanding essential oils used in spiritual quests. Early people of Mexico and South America used Palo Santo to cleanse one's spirit of negative energies. Palo Santo is available as sticks of wood, as an essential oil, incense, and powder.

A good blend to help you develop a higher spiritual consciousness consists of four drops of Palo Santo Essential Oil, 5 drops of Lavender Essential Oil, and five drops of Frankincense. Place these in a diffuser and be sure to follow its directions for operation. Some aromatherapists also suggest using one or two drops of Lemon Balm Essential il. (Sometimes called Melissa Essential Oil)

I take a Palo Santo stick, light it, and waft the smoke throughout a room to refresh the room, to help create a favorable ambiance. Its other uses include relieving cold symptoms, coughs, anxiety, and inflammation. Besides that, it just smells good.

Frankincense is another favorite to aid in improving and or developing spiritual awareness. It is made from the Boswellia Tree and is grown in India and the Arabian Peninsula. The tree has an incision made into its trunk to allow oleoresin, a white milky liquid, to exude. This resin is allowed to harden into an orange-brown gum. This gum is then subjected to steam distillation and turned into an essential oil.

It is famous in the Christian Religion as one of the gifts the Wise Men brought to Jesus at the time of his birth. Frankincense also played a significant role in the religions of Ancient Egypt, Babylon, and Persia. Frankincense Essential Oil promotes acceptance, emotional balance, and stability. Because It develops a clearer focus a broader spiritual awareness becomes a possibility. Frankincense has many medicinal uses such as relief from a bee sting and promoting healthy skin. It helps induce sleep, boost the immune system, and remove negative feelings.

Frankincense is said to reduce joint inflammation, improve asthma, oral health, and gut functions. It is a good antiseptic. However, some people may experience nausea, cramps, and diarrhea when using Frankincense. Those who use cholesterol drugs, blood thinners should avoid using this essential oil

Rosemary's warmth brings comfort and a sense of peace as it enhances natural energy flow. It does this by removing spiritual blocks. It is a wonderful oil to place in a small tub filled with warm water for a foot soak. Sometimes, I place both Cedarwood and Rosemary on a client's feet. I prefer to begin with a client's feet because one's feet are a source of irritation, often pain that affects the whole body. Additionally, many shoes are made of man-made compositions and these can be a source of issues by blocking the natural energies from the earth.

Rosemary is a widely popular essential oil that is used for medicinal purposes. It supports memory and enhances concentration. It clears negative energy, improves circulation, and strengthens your heartbeat. Additionally, Rosemary helps relieve heartburn and flatulence. For some users, it helps bolster self-confidence.

The Rosemary plant is a popular herb and is used in many foods to enhance their flavors.

Place a couple of drops on the bottom of your feet and gently massage. Or place two drops on a wrist and rub your wrists together. Try a Rosemary foot soak. Add a few drops of Lavender Essential Oil along with the Rosemary in your foot soak for a refreshing smell.

Ylang-ylang (pronounced as EE-lang EE-lang) is an evergreen grown in Southeast Asia. It has a spicy sweetness odor. Most of this essential oil is produced in the Comoro Islands, Madagascar, and Réunion.

It is not uncommon for people to feel dis-ease. Often the cause is the lack of an expression of gratitude to friends, family, the Earth, and even to the Universe. Ylang-ylang is excellent to use whenever there is a need to express gratitude. You may also place two drops (if it is in a base oil) about an inch above the eyebrows and in the center to help connect to the Third Eye.

Ylang-ylang Essential Oil is excellent for calming. It helps to relieve stress, anxieties, and hypertension. Quite often, just having two or three drops in a diffuser is sufficient to return you to a calm state. It works to clear heat from the heart when there is serious nervous tension causing palpitations and tachycardia.

Combine a carrier oil such as jojoba, sweet almond, or avocado oil with ylang-ylang to apply directly to the skin. It can also be added to your bath. To aid you in clearing the upper nasal passages add a few drops to a tissue and slowly inhale. Do that a couple of times. Add a few drops of Ylang-ylang to a diffuser to help your breathing.

Ylang-Ylang helps boost one's mood as well as reduce depression and alleviate anxiety. It helps lower blood pressure, decreases the heart rate, and stomach distress. Applied to the impacted areas, Ylang-Ylang helps reduce the pain of rheumatism and gout. Place a couple of drops on your forehead for headaches.

Early cultures believed it enhanced sexual desire.

Do not, and I repeat, do not take ylang-ylang internally. Be sure to test for skin irritation before continued use. Do not use it on cats and dogs.

Lavender has so many wonderful uses which include meditation, calming, soothing the soul, and as a preparation for spiritual enlightenment. Lavender Essential Oil comes in sprays, ointments, candles, and even wipes. It is a wonderful disinfectant. It is an all-around essential oil.

To assist you in your spiritual journey place several drops in a diffuser, burn lavender incense, or place a couple of drops on your wrists and rub them together. If you have trouble falling asleep, place a couple of drops of lavender under your nose or if you have a lavender salve place a small amount of that under your nose, or use a lavender spray on your pillow. During a healing session, I spray a client's feet with lavender to help them relax and I use lavender hydrosol to clean the massage table before and after a client. You can use lavender hydrosol to pre-clean your fruit and vegetables. It is an excellent disinfectant and is good for cleaning countertops. It blends well with several other essential oils.

Lavender Essential Oil is a natural flea repellent and can help keep your dog flea and tick-free. Add a few drops of therapeutic grade Lavender Essential Oil in your dog's shampoo, or dilute it in water to use as a spray. However, according to the ASPCA, lavender is **toxic to cats. Don't use it on cats.**

Tea-Tree essential oil is from a tree named by the famous Captain James Cook, discoverer of New Zealand. Cook is said to have made a spicy tea from the leaves of the tree. Despite its name, Tea-Tree is not connected to the plant for making oolong tea. In 1923, it was discovered that Tea-Tree essential oil was a strong antiseptic and it is now valued for its anti-infectious qualities. It can be used for bacterial, viral, and fungal infections. Tea-Tree Essential Oil can be used to reduce colds, flu, bronchitis, and sinusitis. It helps to reinforce the heart, lungs, and nervous system. Further, it helps the flow of blood to the brain and reduces mental fatigue.

Tea-Tree Essential Oil may be used to help keep skin, hair, and nails healthy. Additionally, Tea-Tree Essential Oil is a good hand sanitizer, insect repellent, natural deodorant, healer for minor cuts, clears acne, and nail fungus.

There are cautions in the use of Tea-Tree Essential Oil. It should never be ingested. Do a skin test with one or two drops and wait at least 24 hours before actual use. If any irritation shows up do not use the oil. Consult your medical doctor. Do not use it on pets.

Hyssop is a shrub common to southern Europe, certain areas of Asia, Russia, and North America. It is used in rituals, culinary and medicinal arts. It strengthens the lungs. Its heat makes it very stimulating. Only four or five drops should be used for a massage. Hyssop Essential Oil helps lessen sagging skin and wrinkles. It helps immune deficiencies, colds, flu, and is a good infection fighter. As excellent protection against negativity, place a single drop on your wrist and gently rub it in. This is helpful if you are placed in a work or social situation in which you may be affected by others' mood swings. Hyssop Essential Oil helps soothe spasmodic muscles and lower fevers. Finally, it sharpens your awareness and consequently opens you to the potential of spirituality.

Negative side effects from Hyssop Essential Oil include a red rash, itchy skin, hives, severe dryness, and peeling of the skin. Sneezing and a runny nose may also result from Hyssop use.

Do not take Hyssop Essential Oil internally.

Again, be sure to consult your medical doctor before using any essential oil. Do a patch test. To do patch tests first wash your forearm. Do not use scented soap. Second, use a clean towel and dry your arm. Third, gently rub three or four drops of the essential oil on a small area of your clean arm. Cover the spot with a piece of gauze. Wait at least twelve hours. Remove the gauze. If the skin is red, itchy, blistered, or swollen do not continue to use that oil. Wash the area with warm water and soap. If there is a problem, see your medical doctor as soon as possible.

Pregnant and or nursing women should avoid using essential oils as should people who have epilepsy. Don't ingest essential oils. Essential oils are not for everyone

Typically, the carrier oil used to reduce the strength of essential oils is jojoba. Other carrier oils are almond oil, and Macadamia or Argon oils. If you use an oil that should not be used full strength, use one of the previously mentioned carrier oils and about 5% of the pure essential oil.

Spikenard Essential Oil has been around for centuries and is used in religious ceremonies and for physical health purposes. In addition, to being an excellent medicinal tool, its earthy scent makes it a much sought-after perfumery base.

Spikenard is also known as Jatamansi and is a close relative to the Valerian plant. As such, it may help promote mood and emotional health. Spikenard Essential Oil is said to reduce neuroinflammation and as a result may improve one's anxiety, depression, and stress. Place a couple of drops in a diffuser.

As an anti-inflammatory and antibacterial, Spikenard may also help with athlete's foot, dandruff, muscle and joint pain, migraine, and gastrointestinal problems. However, this oil as well as other essential oils may cause itchiness and skin irritations such as hives and rashes, boils, and peeling of the skin. *Do not place it near your eyes.*

Spikenard Essential Oil may also be used in the bath. Use no more than a tablespoon to the tub while warm water is running.

Vetiver Essential Oil is made from Vetiver grass and is also called Khus Oil. It comes from India. It has an earthy scent. Unlike some other essential oils, Vetiver roots are used only after they have been aged. Once aged, the plant roots are soaked in water. When the oil is released into the water, it is skimmed off the top.

Vetiver Essential Oils is useful in removing mental fatigue; thus, improving mental alertness. Place two or three drops of the oil in a diffuser in your work area. Speaking of diffusers, place one with Vetiver Essential Oil in it, in your bedroom to help relieve heavy snoring. Be sure the diffuser automatically shuts off.

If you suffer from chronic anxiety place two drops of Vetiver Essential Oil on a wrist. Rub your two wrists together for a couple of seconds. A cautionary reminder is appropriate here. Before you use any essential oil on your skin, do a patch test. If you detect any irritation consult with your medical doctor before continuing.

For ticks, the culprit in Lyme Disease, Vetiver is highly toxic. Use Vetiver in a carrier oil and apply it directly to your skin. A 2015 study reported in Trusted Sources indicates Vetiver Essential Oil may be more effective than some of the commercial products.

If you can't buy Vetiver Essential Oil already mixed with a carrier oil you can mix your own. Use jojoba oil, macadamia oil, walnut oil, olive oil, or avocado oil. (Be sure there are no issues using one of the 'nut' oils.) Mix two drops of Vetiver Oil in every 10 drops of the carrier oil and apply to the skin. If you find no negative reaction you can add more drops of Vetiver to the carrier oil.

Sage Essential Oil can be made from Spanish Sage or Common Sage also called True Sage, Garden Sage, and Dalmatian Sage. Sage has a long history of being used for medicinal purposes such as coughs, asthma, bronchitis, angina, inflammation, depression, circulation issues, and emotional problems such as depression.

The word sage comes from the Latin word *sapere* which means "to save." In this case, to save the users' health. Among the many uses of Sage Essential Oil two will be presented here: massage and hair treatment.

Sage Essential Oil combined with these essential oils; lime, grapefruit, and thyme essential oils. Combine 10 to 12 drops of each of these oils add them to two ounces of carrier oil in a clean glass bottle, secure the cap and mix well. A trick I learned from my aromatherapist I think will work well with this essential oil mixture. Before applying the essential oil to your skin, take the bottle, hold it in your dominant hand, making sure your fingers are wrapped around the bottle. Don't squeeze the bottle. The reason for doing this is to energize the oil with your energy; thus, making it more effective.

For a hair treatment that is said to thicken the hair combine two ounces of Macadamia Oil or Sweet Almond Oil with one ounce of Jojoba oil in an 8-ounce glass measuring cup. In a pan, bring two cups of water to a boil, remove from the heat, insert the measuring cup containing the essential oil. Leave it in the water just long enough to warm; make sure it is not too hot to apply. Add 30 drops of Essential Sage Oil and 15 drops of Ylang-Ylang Essential Oil, blend well. Gently massage the essential oils into the scalp, making sure the stands are well coated. Cover the head with a shower cap and leave it on for 30 minutes. Use a regular shampoo to wash out the oils and towel dry. If you use an electric hair dryer do so on low heat. Do this at least once a week. If any issues arise, stop using it and consult your medical doctor immediately.

With the contemporary concern about mental alacrity, it is well to remember that sage has a long history as a treatment for mental decline. Common and Spanish Sage essential oils may help improve memory and cognition. The natural antioxidant and anti-inflammatory properties of these oils may prevent the progression of dementia.

Warning: Sage oils should not be ingested. There is a risk of poisoning. Even small amounts of Sage Essential Oil ingested by children have caused seizures. There is the possibility of an allergic reaction such as itchiness, tingling of the fingers, shortness of breath. hives, and dizziness. There is the potential of a severe reaction that may lead to anaphylaxis. Additionally, if you have a history of cancer, heart issues, skin disorders, hormone issues, epilepsy, or high blood pressure you are urged to consult your medical doctor before using Sage Oil. Never apply Sage Oil near the eyes.

Essential Oils and Crystals: Can you use essential oils with crystals? Yes, it is one way of increasing the "power" or "value" of both the oil and the crystal. Here are the steps to follow to create a crystal-infused essential oil.

1. Set your clear and specific intention.

2. Choose the crystal that is a natural aid to that intention.

3. Select the essential oil that helps strengthen your intention.

4. Be sure you clean your crystal, and have a small clean bottle with a cap,

5. Place the crystal or pieces of a crystal to the bottle,

6. Add 3 or 4 drops of the essential oil of choice and then fill the bottle the rest of the way up with a base oil such as jojoba, macadamia nut oil, almond oil, or avocado oil. (If you have 'nut' allergies do not use a nut-based base oil) You can also use Olive oil.

7. Let the oil and crystal rest for 24 hours.

8. Place a single drop on each wrist or behind each ear.

Here is a shortlist of essential oils and suggest crystals to pair:

*Frankincense paired with Amethyst is used for confidence and protection

*Ylang-ylang paired with Rose Quartz for love

*Hyssop paired with Tourmaline for inspiration and compassion

*Patchouli paired with Citrine for creativity

*Tea Tree Essential Oil paired with Clear Quartz for healing

*Lavender paired with Chrysocolla for peace and compassion

*Vetiver paired with Blue Calcite for trust

*Sage paired with a Herkimer Diamond for self-appreciation

Patchouli Essential Oil comes from Southeast Asia and the Tamil people. The word patchouli means green leaf. The plant grows to 36 inches tall. The plant's leaves and stems are harvested and allowed to dry and essential oil is extracted using a distillation process. Patchouli Essential Oil goes well with Sandalwood, Jasmine, and Rose oils. Its smell is best described as woody, a bit sweet, and spicy. Besides its use as an additive in perfume, Patchouli Essential Oil has other important uses as well.

1. Ground Patchouli leaves added to hot water makes a tea to aid in digestion issues.

2. Used to treat skin irritations such as dermatitis, acne, dry skin

3. Relieves systems of headaches, stomach upset, colds

4. Relieves depression

5. Helps one to relax and to ease stress and anxiety

6. Helps with oily hair and dandruff

7. Helps control appetite

8. Used as an insecticide, antifungal, or antibacterial agent

9. It may be added to foods as a flavoring in small amounts

10. Used in a bath to relieve pain from rheumatism.

Always error on the side of caution when using any supportive medicine. Because Patchouli Essential Oil can affect blood clotting people who are taking blood-thinners, who have had recent major surgery or will be doing so, and those with bleeding disorders such as hemophilia should AVOID using Patchouli Essential Oil.

At this point research to support the use of Patchouli is small with most of the support being anecdotal, however, research is increasing and is showing some benefits in using Patchouli Essential Oil. Recent studies are listed in the References at the end of this book.

Two areas of physical concern are care of one's skin and what to do about wrinkles. Essential oils may provide help for dry skin or its opposite, oily skin and sensitive skin. Additionally, one of the areas that receive a good deal of cosmetic promotion is wrinkles.

Essential Oils for dry skin include Lavender, Chamomile, and Sandalwood. Because of its anti-inflammatory qualities, Lavender Essential Oil helps reduce redness and because it is known as a natural hydrator, Lavender Essential Oil can return the much-needed moisture to the dry skin. An additional bonus of Lavender Essential Oils, besides its aroma, is it is not overly greasy. As far as the use of Chamomile is concerned you may want to avoid it if you have allergies. Besides smelling good, Sandalwood promotes skin moisture.

If you suffer oily skin Clary Sage helps control the excess sebum on your skin; thus, making it less oily. Rosemary, Neroli, and Frankincense are good for controlling excessive oil.

For suffers from acne, Rosemary and Frankincense help reduce microbials.

Applying undiluted essential oils to the skin may irritate. If you experience any skin irritation from using any of the essential oils stop all applications and consult your medical doctor.

Wrinkles 101 anyone? Commercials on television and promotional ads on various social media are loaded with antiwrinkle lotions, serums, and creams, and these are not just aimed at women. Many of these products are very expensive and those that are not brought into question their effectiveness. There are essential oils that will help lessen wrinkles. They do not get rid of them! According to the American Academy of Dermatology, it can take up to three months for a new skincare routine to take effect. Keep your expectations reasonable. If you have an issue using any of these essential oils stop their use and see your medical doctor.

Rosemary Essential Oil in a carrier oil may benefit your skin's overall condition. Gently apply 1 drop daily to the area you want to reduce wrinkles. Do this after your shower and before going to bed.

Lemon Essential Oil is an antioxidant and is high in Vitamin C. Use sparingly and do not go out in the sun immediately after application. Apply 1 drop to the wrinkled area. Do this daily just before bedtime.

Neroli Essential Oil according to the National Center for Complementary and Integrative Health, Neroli can help a variety of skin issues. In terms of wrinkles, it is believed that Neroli Essential Oil helps rebuild the skin's elasticity and may help generate new skin cells thus reducing wrinkles. The one-drop rule applies to this essential oil. Apply before bedtime.

These oils may also help reduce skin wrinkles: Sandalwood, Geranium, Ylang-Ylang, and Helichrysum.

CHAPTER EIGHT
CRYSTALS AND THEIR USES

Besides being a shaman, I am a certified crystal healer. I use crystals as a part of my healing practice. In this class, I will provide a brief informational background about crystals and then move right into specific crystals and their uses in healing.

Remember, healing encompasses the physical, mental, and emotional aspects of the human being, and by physical, I mean the actual physical body; mental refers to the processes involved in the brain, and by emotional, I mean feelings. Further, I believe these three areas are linked and as such, my emphasis is on the whole person.

The use of stones has been used for thousands of years. They have been warmed to bring pain relief and for cooking. Exactly how long they have been used in healing is a question of debate. Crystals have been around for a very long time as decorations and as instruments to aid healing. Some authorities indicate stones that look like "ice" has been used for at least 6,000 years. Certainly, early humankind did not call these "pretty" shiny stones crystals. The word crystal has been recorded back in the 1300s. Archaeological records indicate that crystals were used ornamentally in Ancient Egypt, by the Mayans and the Incas. However, there is evidence in a hieroglyphic papyrus dated 1500 BC indicating crystals were used for medical purposes. Whatever the timeframe, crystals have become a mainstay of modern metaphysical pursuits and supportive medicine.

Turquoise was revered by the Tibetans, Quartz by the Japanese, and Jade held sway with the early Chinese. The ancient culture of India used crystals in human energy centers (chakras). For them, the Moonstone, Onyx, and Ruby were important in personal relationships.

The First Settlers of South, Central, and North America used crystals for spiritual, ceremonial, and healing purposes. There is evidence that crystals had a practical use as well. For example, obsidian made a good cutting tool and pyrite was used as mirrors by the early Mexicans.

As for the word crystal itself, it comes from the Ancient Greek word, *krustallos* meaning "ice." Crystals are molecular; may be colored or clear, and are found all over the world.

In the 1970s a renaissance created by the New Age Culture brought the use of crystals for medicinal purposes to new heights. Stores specializing in gemstones and crystals have spread from one American coast to the other. And as with other things, you get what you pay for. The question arises about scientific evidence that supports the notion that crystals heal. I know of none. However, Christopher French and his colleagues at Goldsmiths College, the University of London back in 2001, did a study of 80 participants. They found no evidence to support a positive effect in healing beyond that of a placebo effect. There are studies about crystal vibrations and for me, therein, lays their value in healing. Everything vibrates; for example, the human body vibrates between 62 to 70 Hz and it is a vibration that creates energy. Crystals' vibrational modes are called Phonons. And these can be measured. Add the fact that the flow of vibrations in humans, animals, and plants can also be measured; it seems, then, that there is a basis for determining a change in vibrations when crystals are applied.

As a shamanic healer, I use crystals in three ways: placing them on the client, surrounding the client with various crystals, and crystal elixirs. If, for example, a client's issues are primarily emotional, I will place a Rose Quartz crystal in the individual's left hand. Next, I will place a Pink Magano calcite on the individual's left shoulder, and finally Morganite by the left ear. Each of these crystals relates to the heart chakra. I place them on the left side as it puts them closest to the heart. On the other hand, if the client is experiencing physical pain, a different set of crystals is used. For example, if the client has shoulder pain, I have them lay face down on the massage table and place three clear quartz crystals on the distressed shoulder. Just below the shoulder, I place Amethyst and Selenite; both are excellent for pain relief.

Crystal elixirs provide another avenue of support for the immune system. However, not all crystals are safe to use for an elixir. Some estimates of unsafe crystals are as high as 45. Those crystals you should not use for elixirs include Alexandrite, Aventurine, Chrysocolla, Garnet, Hematite, Labradorite, Lapis Lazuli, Selenite, Sodalite, Sugilite, and Tourmaline.

To create your crystal elixir, first sterilize a quart glass bottle, including its top. This does not mean just running it under hot water. Place the glass bottle in boiling water and do so for at least four minutes. Once the bottle is cool, fill the bottle with distilled water. In a bowl, large enough to hold the quart bottle, place the bottle in the center of the bowl, fill the bowl with tap water, but not enough to overflow. In this bowl, place two clear quartz crystals or two amethyst crystals or a combination. These should be about the size of a quarter. Cover the top of the quart jar with a piece of gauze. Let this sit for 48 hours. Remove the quart bottle from the bowl, remove the gauze, put the lid on the bottle, and refrigerate overnight. Discard the water in the bowl. Drink two ounces of the crystal elixir a day. The length of time you should drink the crystal elixir depends upon your issues. I mention the Quartz and Amethyst Elixir because it is the one, I prepared for my wife who was fighting a rare form of bone cancer. It's good support for the immune system.

Sometimes clients ask what effects crystal elixirs have. Unlike herbal and essential oil sprays and salves, the elixirs work inside the body. Besides being good for hydration, crystal elixirs are effective for constipation, for relief of aching muscles, and of course for external uses such as cuts and sore feet. An Amber Crystal Elixir is suggested for mild constipation and an Aragonite Crystal Elixir helps get relief from aching muscles. For your home use, you can make an elixir in the amount that would last you several days; however, I do not make them in advance. After a client session, I may say I will make a crystal elixir for them and they would have to come back in two days to pick it up.

Again, please check with your medical doctor before using any supportive medical approach. You will hear me say this over and over throughout the book.

I'm often asked how you know which crystal you should buy. Generally, the first answer is a simple one: If you are attracted to the crystal, then select that one. The attraction may involve color and shape. The second one and one which I feel supports the first is how the crystal feels. Pick up a crystal, hold it in the palm of your hand, and loosely close your fingers around the crystal. Do not squeeze the crystal. You will feel the pulse in your fingers and not the energy emitted by the crystal. What will your feeling be? You might feel a slight vibration—a pulsing, or warmth emanating from the crystal. You may feel nothing. And that's not an indication that there is something wrong with you. So, what do you do? Try another crystal, even several. If you do not sense the crystal there may be several reasons for this. First, someone may have handled the crystal that had a lot of negativities, or several people with negative energy walked around the store, and finally, the crystal itself, may have had trouble reading you because you were tense, nervous, or feeling insecure. Buy the crystal which attracted you. Take it home, place it on your nightstand, next day place it on your desk where you work, or slip it in your pocket or purse. Give it a chance to tune into your vibrations.

Because of the huge number of crystals existing in the world, only a few will be considered here. These include the powerful Shaman Stone, the unwashable stone, Quartz, Agate, Tourmaline, Obsidian, Amethyst, Cavansite, Boji Stone, Rose Quartz, and Blue Calcite, Chrysocolla, Citrine, Herkimer Diamond, Sodalite.

MOQUI BALLS

The Shaman's Stone also goes by the names Moqui Balls and Moqui Marbles. Found in Utah and Arizona, the Shaman's Stone is a rich chocolate-colored rock made of iron oxide, sandstone, and an outer shell of Hematite. The estimated age of the Shaman Stone is 300,000 years old to 25 million years old. Because they are from the earth, these stones are said to be among the most energetic materials on earth. Note the phrase "on earth." The Moqui Marbles lay on top of the ground and because they do, it is said they are useful in moving negative energy from the body and grounding it to the earth.

Having high vibration, this stone helps remove energy blockages, used to relieve pain. As a consequence, one's Chakras are cleared and brought into alignment. Once the negative energy has been removed, the Shaman's Stone helps to transfer positive energy from the etheric to the actual physical body, helps to heal emotional problems.

One of the characteristics that make Moqui Marbles unique is that they come as male and female and are generally used together in healing sessions. The female stone is smooth; whereas, the male stone has a rougher outside and may also be a bit larger.

The Shaman's Stone is also an excellent tool in meditation. Hold one or both of the balls in your hands. Take several deep breaths and move into your preferred meditation mode.

Selenite, the unwashable stone, is a crystallized

form of gypsum. Selenite has six other names. These are satin spar, desert rose, gypsum flower, butterfly selenite, golden phantom, and disodium selenite. By whatever name it is called, Selenite is a powerful healing stone. It is one of a few crystals that do not need to be charged per se. By that, I mean it does not have to be placed in the sunlight or moonlight to activate its energy. However, because numerous people may have handled the piece you purchased it should be cleansed. First, it should never be placed in any liquid. It will dissolve. Here are three things you can do to cleanse your selenite crystal:

1.Use a smudge stick, either white mountain sage or Palo Santo, and pass the Selenite through the smoke several times.

2.Place the Selenite close to an Mp3 file of vibration or near a singing bowl. Leave the crystal near the sound for 3 minutes.

3.Place the Selenite in a glass bowl filled ¾ with dry salt. I prefer Himalayan salt. Leave the crystal in the bowl for at least 2 hours, turning the crystal every 30 minutes.

Selenite is often used to cleanse other crystals. Place the crystals on a clean surface and add the Selenite for twenty-four hours.

It is said to be an excellent conduit for connecting to spirit guides and the spirit world. I recommend a polished Selenite wand. It does not leave a white residue on your skin or clothing. Hold the crystal in your dominant hand and use whatever approach you normally use to move into an altered state of consciousness to seek your Spirit Guide.

The wand should come to a point and that plays an important role in healing. The Selenite may also be pyramidal. If you have a place on your body that is giving you pain, place the point of the Selenite on that spot, and hold it there for a couple of minutes. Give it a light pressure. Then turn the crystal around, using the rounded or flattened end to gently massage the area of pain.

Selenite also helps clear blocked energy paths, provides clarity of thinking, supports intuition, and increases positive energy. To rid yourself of negativity, take a Selenite Wand and do a sweep of each arm. Begin at the shoulder and sweep the Wand to the end of your fingertips. Do this three times on each arm.

Quartz, probably the most widely known stone, is a master crystal and is the most abundant mineral found on Earth. It is resistant to both mechanical and chemical weathering. On the Mohs Scale, it registers 7 in terms of hardness. Topaz, Corundum, and Diamond are harder, Diamond being the hardest of all minerals. What then is Clear Quartz Crystal? It is a transparent stone composed of silicon and oxygen. Probably the one feature of quartz is its ability to vibrate and to do so at precise frequencies. Quartz has a Hz frequency of 32,768, that is, it vibrates 32,768 times per second. A hertz means the crystal vibrates one cycle per minute. It is this very high vibrational quality that makes quartz useful in watches and equipment that transmits radio and television signals. Quartz crystals are used in electronic games, computers, cell phones, and GPS equipment. If it can do that, just think about what it can do for the physical, mental, and emotional aspects of the human body. Vibration is a source of healing.

Besides Clear Quartz there are six additional kinds of quartz: Rose Quartz Tiger's Eye Quartz, Citrine Quartz, Snow Quartz, Smoky Quartz, and Ametrine Quartz.

Quartz is a wonderful stone for helping with spirituality. To enhance your spiritual awareness, place several pieces of clear quartz in the room in which you spend most of your time; place a couple of pieces by your nightstand, or place two or three small pieces in a little bag and tuck that under your pillow at night. If you are already high spiritual, the quartz will act as a beacon, a bridge for connecting to the spiritual world, to spirit animals and plants. Not only is quartz helpful in communicating with that which is spiritual, but it is also an excellent aid in person-to-person communication. If you and a loved one are having issues, hold a piece of quartz to talk with them via telephone, cellphone, or one of the visuals such as Skype or FaceTime, or Zoom.

In terms of one's physical well-being, quartz has been used for thousands of years. It helps heal several conditions that negatively impact one's physical health. Because of its high vibrancy, quartz help to improve the circulatory system, it stimulates the immune system and calms the nervous system. It relieves pain from burns and reduces blistering. On a personal note, I will share with you one experience with Clear Quarts' healing powers. My niece and her friend had come to visit my wife and me. I decided to do the man thing and grill steaks. Once they were done, I placed the steaks on a clean plater to take into the house. I turned and reached out to close the lid on the grill. I missed the lid and my hand went directly on the hot, still flaming grill. I hurried into the house, steak platter still in hand, went into my office, grabbed quartz crystal, and held it in my hand. The searing pain stopped and no blisters formed. Oh, by the way, everyone enjoyed the steaks, including me.

If you have made a quartz elixir it can be applied to the skin to reduce the itching or to soothe sunburn.

Another use of clear quartz is in the area of personal meditation. It helps you to filter out what I call "brain noise." This is simply the self-chatter we all do. Holding a piece of clear quartz helps to bring your intention to full focus. You may wish to place clear quartz into a grid or to place a piece on an altar in front of which you can sit. Add Pink Petalite with clear quartz to increase the depth of your meditation.

If you are experiencing negative emotional issues, add to the clear quartz, Petalite whether it is gray, blue, green, or pink. Place a couple of pieces of each in a small pouch and wear it around your neck. During a healing session in which the drum plays a significant role, I place several pieces of Petalite around the client's body to increase the positive vibration.

To help you during sleep time, place Clear Quartz or any one of the other six quartzes in a small cloth bag and place it under your pillow.

Quartz needs to be cleaned and keeping it clean helps to ensure its effectiveness. Place your crystal in the sun for one hour or leave it in the moonlight overnight. You can cleanse your crystal with warm water and mild soap. Be sure to rinse thoroughly.

One more thing about Quartz. As is far too often the case, some try to take advantage of others. How do you tell if your crystal is the real deal? Take your Quartz Crystal and hold it over a piece of writing. Real Quartz magnifies or distorts the writing. That's a good sign it's real.

MOSS AGATE
01/07/20

Agate is a microcrystalline-quartz mineraloid and is formed over thousands of years. It is a type of Chalcedony. The one pictured is Moss Agate. Like other crystals, the Agate comes in various colors and a wide variety of striations. It is an excellent crystal for raising self-awareness, transforming negative energy, and healing anger, sadness, and lack of self-worth. Agate improves one's mental processes which results in clarity of thought. By the way, if you are a student and have issues with testing, carry a piece of Agate with you.

Lace Agate types are usually flat and contain swirls and concentric circles that compose intricate patterns that resemble lace; thus, its name. In addition to Lace Agate, there are 18 other types of Agate Crystals. These include Turritella, Carnelian, Coldwater, Greek Achates, Fire Agate, Brazilian, Polyhedroid, Botswana, Plume, Condor Holley Blue, Moss, Tube, Fortification, Lake Superior, Binghamite, Patuxent River, and Enhydro Agate.

The Agate enhances mental function, improves concentration, enhances the perception and analytical abilities and as such, it helps to bring about personal harmony and balance. It is a soothing gemstone that heals inner anger, anxiety and helps in the strengthening of relationships.

Tourmaline is known as the grounding crystal. Discovered in the 17th Century its name comes from the Sinhalese[viii] word "turmali" which means unknown stone of different colors. The colors range from blue to pink to rose to black. It is an excellent combatant against negative energy. It's an all-around crystal of protection even though most are very black.

Tourmaline. Especially Black Tourmaline has excellent healing properties. It helps strengthen the immune system; eases joint pain, stress, and tension. If you have a fellow worker who has issues Tourmaline is an excellent crystal to help promote sympathy or if you have a fear of something, carry a piece of Tourmaline with you. If you or someone you know has panic attacks, Tourmaline can help soothe that inner conflict. If you are in the business of helping people heal, keep a couple of Tourmaline crystals in your studio to bring their healing qualities to yourself.

If you are experiencing negative vibrations caused by "evil" spirits, soul loss, or soul-entanglement you have an outstanding stone of protection in Tourmaline. Wear a necklace made of

Black Tourmaline, carry a piece in your pocket, purse, or briefcase, place several pieces throughout your office and home.

Another bonus of adding Tourmaline to your life is that it helps promote equality between men and women not only in the workplace but in their social life. To reap the many benefits of Tourmaline, no matter its color, and in addition to carrying a piece with you, take a Tourmaline Crystal and gently rub it on your skin.

A Tourmaline Crystal is a wonderful symbol. It reminds us that despite the divisive issues in society and our daily lives, like the undertone of colors in the Tourmaline that merge to create a thing of beauty, we too, can come together.

The Tourmaline should be cleaned regularly. No soap; just warm water and a dry cloth for drying are all that is necessary. After each cleansing, recharge the crystal by placing it in the moonlight overnight. If leaving your crystal outdoors, place it in a box with Selenite and Clear Quartz.

As with other crystals, Tourmaline should be programmed. Once your stone has been cleansed you can reprogram it. To do so, follow these simple steps:

1. Make sure the crystal is dry.

2. Hold the crystal in your dominant hand. Do not squeeze the crystal.

3. Let the crystal adjust to your skin and body temperature. This should take about 2 minutes.

4. Be sure you are seated. Slowly close your eyes. Don't squeeze them shut.

5. Relax and allow your thoughts to flow, undeveloped. Allow your mind and body to meld; forgetting you are holding a crystal.

6. Do this for 5 minutes. Slowly open your eyes. Return the crystal to its place.

BLACK OBSIDIAN
01.02.2008

Obsidian which holds a special place in my personal and professional life is among the few crystals known to have been used throughout human history. It first came to the world's stage in a written commentary in 77 AD when Pliny the Elder mentioned it in his book, *Natural History*. Obsidian is an extremely strong and reflective crystal formed from molten lava that has been cooled so quickly it didn't have time to form into glass. Because it comes from the womb of Mother Earth, it is a very power-driven crystal. It aids in personal and group protection, grounding (stabilizing and emotional rollercoaster), and helps promote Spiritual communication. An Obsidian crystal may be black, green, purple, brown, blue, or what is called rainbow.

Some writers refer to the Black Obsidian as a "psychic vacuum cleaner"[1] because it sucks out all the negativity and junk floating around in one's auric field. In doing so, it creates a powerful shield

---

e[1] Mentioned in Crystaline Wellness. Com. Au.

against negativity, psychic attacks, and attempts to interfere with the Soul. The basic healing properties of Obsidians fall into 7 layers:

1.Purification- Removal of contaminants; to make one clean

2.Transformation- Modification of the energy of the auric field

3.Fulfillment- Brings into existence that which fulfills or satisfies

4.Metamorphoses- Changes all aspects of a sense of worth

5.Manifestation- Releases incarnation of spiritual qualities

6.Practicality- Holds auric energy inline

7.Psychic Ability- Opens the door for otherworldly experiences

The pendulum I use is an Obsidian crystal arrowhead wrapped in silver wire. It is attached to a seven-inch silver chain with an obsidian ball at its other end. I use it to measure the energy level of clients as well as a connector to the Spirit World.

In addition to being a helpmate to the Spirit World, the Black Tourmaline is an excellent aid in meditation. Before you begin to meditate be sure you have cleansed and recharged your Black Tourmaline Crystal. Find a quiet and comfortable place where you will not be disturbed for several minutes. Turn on a battery-powered candle. Select music or sound for meditation. Turn it on, just loud enough to be heard. Placing your crystal depends on how you are positioned. If you are seated in a yoga position, place the crystal on the floor directly in front of your crossed legs. If you are lying down, place the crystal on your forehead and if you are seated in a chair, hold the crystal in your dominant hand. Begin whatever breathing technique you use and count from 15 to 0. Close your eyes as you steady your breathing.

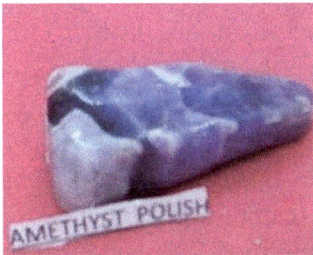

Amethyst, on the Mohs Scale, registers a hardness of 7, is found in Brazil, Bolivia, Mexico, Canada, Russia, Europe, and the United States. Archaeological evidence tells us that Amethyst has been used for a variety of purposes for 25,000 years ago. And like the many years of its being used, its uses are wide and varied. Early The Greek word for Amethyst is ametusthos which means "not intoxicated" and they believed Amethyst inhibited intoxication; whereas, the Chinese believed it brought prosperity and the Ancient Egyptians used it to protect themselves from witchcraft. Today, healers use Amethyst to help their clients create harmony, sharpen intuition, relieve anxiety, to meditate, and boost their immune systems. Without question, Amethyst is the most popular of the Quartz clan and by many, it is viewed as the most powerful and protective of all crystals.

In addition to inhibiting intoxication, bringing prosperity, and providing protection against witchcraft there are five other significant healing qualities:

1.Insomnia is reduced and memory of dreams is improved

2.Activates intuition, enhances psychic abilities, and acts as a cleansing agent

3.Boosts one's immune system

4.Relieves stress, hypertension, and angst.

The following five Amethyst are known for their extra healing powers:

1.Ametrine Amethyst promotes creativity, insights and is an excellent healing crystal

2.Brandberg Amethyst is an excellent healing crystal that helps restore one's purpose

3.Cacoxenite Amethyst encourages creativity, innovation, experimentation, and spirituality

4.Chevron Amethyst enhances introspection, opens spiritual channels as it repels negativity

5.Espiritu Santo Rutilated Amethyst is a rare crystal that helps spiritual awakening, develops psychic abilities, helps connect to the higher realm.

Amethyst should be kept in a dark storage drawer or jewelry box. Do not place in direct sunlight or bright artificial light. Moderate temperature only.

Programming an Amethyst means activating its energy. Do not place it in the sun or leave it out for moonlight. The three-step program:

1.Have a specific intention

2.Hold the Amethyst in your dominant hand, gently close your fingers around the crystal

3.Hold the crystal in your cupped hand over your heart. This will open the third eye and then hold the crystal on your third eye to lock your intention. (The Third Eye is located between your eyebrows, about an inch up in the center.)

Place Amethyst Crystals throughout your home, office, car, and carry them on your person, or place it under your pillow. Amethyst is good for clearing negative energy and it is an excellent addition to a Clear Quartz Elixir to aid in strengthening the immune system.

When I have a client that is highly tense and anxious, I place them in a meditative state. An amethyst is placed in each of the person's hands, one on each side of the head, and one in the center of the head, between the eyebrows. I play one of two CDs: One that is soft drumming and the other an Mp3 at 396 Mhz. The lights are soft and lavender incense is burned. After 15 minutes, I take up the drum and by increasing the beat I bring the person out of the meditative state. As an aside, always clean the amethyst after a healing session. Place it next to the Selenite for 30 minutes. Selenite is an excellent cleaner for all other crystals.

CAVANCITE

Cavansite is another stone for your consideration. It is a powerful energy crystal composed of *ca*lcium, *van*adium, and *silicate*. Thus, its name is made up of the first letters of each of these minerals. This deep blue crystal was first found in the state of Oregon in 1967. It was also found in the countries of India, New Zealand, and Brazil. It embraces humanity and oneness including the divine within each of us. It helps us to remember we are all connected to something powerful and pure. It helps you make sense of past experiences.

Cavansite will help you with courage and confidence, especially during periods of transitions in your lifestyle. It will help reinforce your self-esteem and reassure you that your knowledge and actions are on the right path.

Hold a piece of Cavansite as an aid to your meditation or slip a piece under your pillow at night for dream clarity. During sessions with your Spirit Guide, Cavansite will enhance your communication. It sharpens your intuitions. If you have suffered a loss, this crystal will help you process your grief.

Cavansite is said to help with problems with the following: Eyes, throat, bladder, kidney, tinnitus, blood disorders stimulate the endocrine system, and relieve headaches.

Cavansite: will help you in your daily meditations

will also help you sleep soundly when you are experiencing sleep troubles.

will also remove your stress and anxieties.

will allow you to relax

will help you have a moment of peace in your busy daily life.

will be an aide in smoothing out tense talks at home or the workplace.

The Boji Stone[2] is not the same as the Moqui 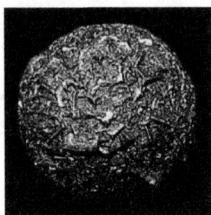 Stone. The Boji is composed of Palladium, Pyrite, Petrified Bone, and Fossils. Moqui Marbles are composed of sand and iron. Boji Stones are large; whereas, Moqui is not. Boji comes from Kansas and Australia; Moqui is from Utah.

Boji comes in pairs, male and female. The male stone has straw-like particles on its surface, the female is smooth. Both are dark brown. Because they possess strong grounding and healing qualities they work well in the arena of the metaphysical. They may be used in a physical body layout, in a prayer circle, or on an altar.

---

[2] The Name Boji is copyrighted as well as trademarked. Only stones from the owner of the copyright and trademark may be sold under that name, Boji.

The Boji is an excellent healer and protector. It helps fix emotional issues, and for those who may feel they have left-over hypnotic suggestions lingering in their psyche grab the Boji Stones hold on to them, place them on your person or under your pillow at night.

The following symptoms may suggest you are ungrounded: dizziness, forgetfulness, a sense you are generally not well, clumsiness, continually slipping off into daydreaming, bright light bothers you, or unable to remain focused. If this is the case, lay down, place the male stone above your head and the female Boji at your feet. I prefer placing the male stone on my client's forehead and the female Boji Stone on the client's lower abdomen. Because the Boji possesses a subtle vibration leave the stones in place for at least 15 minutes.

If you suffer back pain lay on your stomach and have the Boji Stones placed on the area of pain. Fifteen to twenty minutes is a good amount of time. Longer if you need it. If you have arthritis in your hands hold the male stone in your dominant hand; the female stone in the other. Gently close your fingers around the stones. Let your arms dangle down from your chair for five minutes, then rest your hands on your chair arm for five minutes. Do this whenever you need immediate temporary relief.

Rose Quartz is one of the most popular crystals and probably because it is the stone of unconditional love. Historically, we know it has been used as far back as 7,000 BCE. The elite women of Egypt and Rome used Rose Quartz Face

Masks to improve their complexions and to prevent wrinkles.

Rose Quartz Crystals are found in the United States, Australia, Brazil, South Africa, Sweden, Germany, India, and Madagascar.

In addition to being the crystal of unconditional love, Rose Quartz is said to be a powerful healing crystal. It helps heal relationship issues by promoting mutual understanding, kindness, and compassion. In conjunction with relationship issues, Rose Quartz boosts inner peace and self-love.

Create a Rose Quartz Crystal Spray to enhance your space, in your automobile, or on your body. To create the spray, do the following:

1.Add several very small pieces of Rose Quartz to a spray bottle.

2.Using distilled water or filtered tap water, fill the bottle almost to the top. Leave space for air.

3.Insert the sprayer and secure it.

4.Let this rest for 24 hours. This allows the crystal's qualities to diffuse into the water.

5.Once the 24 hours are up, hold the spray bottle in your hand; don't squeeze or hold the bottle tight. Just gently wrap your fingers around the bottle. This allows your energy to mix with the charged crystal water.

6.Lightly spray your area, including yourself. Enjoy.

When worn or carried in a pocket, Rose Quartz blocks negativity. This crystal can be used in rituals, placed under your pillow (place them in a cloth or plastic bag), placed throughout your home or office, held during meditation, or gently rubbed over your face, hands, and arms as part of your skincare routine.

Blue Calcite is a facilitator. It is said to enhance the Maslow "aha" experience and to promote inner vision, psychic ability, astral travel, and shamanic journeying. Blue Calcite is also a powerful stone when it comes to emotional issues. It helps the body to relax, calm emotions, and offers up mental protection. Furthermore, Blue Calcite is very protective when it comes to your aura.

Serving as a sponge, Blue Calcite soaks up all the negative energy and vibrations you encounter and releases them as positive energy. Certainly, a significant fringe benefit of using Blue Calcite is an enhancement of your dream life; thus, rendering clarity. Place a piece of Blue Calcite under your pillow at night.

Citrine is often referred to as the "stone of summer." Its bright lemon-yellow grabs you and holds you in its positive vibrations and gives you that needed burst of energy. If you are experiencing a tough time, hold a piece of Citrine Crystal in your hand, place it on the Third Eye for a few seconds, or gently rub the back of your neck to relieve stress and strain.

Speaking of the Third Eyes brings to mind the metaphysical connection Citrine Crystal brings: It is connected to the Solar Plexus and the Sacral Chakras that help us stay grounded.

As with Crystals, you should keep your Citrine clean. Admittedly, Citrine is one of the stones that sakes off toxic energy. A cleaning, especially if you use it with clients, is always a good idea. Use slightly warm water and mild soap. Rinse the crystal thoroughly, and completely dry the crystal with a clean towel. I do not recommend "charging" Citrine in the sun. Too much heat is not good. If you feel there should be some charging place the crystal at the base of a yellow candle, light the candle, and let it burn for 10 minutes. DANGER! Be very careful of a burning candle. In the everyday busy world, it is all too easy to forget and fire could result. I suggest you set a timer.

Chrysocolla is the teaching, communicating, and transforming crystal. Green in color with a copper undertone, this crystal helps you connect with your sense of wonderment and curiosity.

Chrysocolla helps with guilt, anxiety, depression, self-doubt, and other limiting beliefs that tend to hold you back from accomplishing all that you wish. For you who continue to struggle with grief, heartache created by relationship issues, job and career disappointment Chrysocolla is said to offer the necessary insights to enable movement forward.

The exquisite radiant energy emitted by Chrysocolla brings balance to one's soul; thus, a serene peace. If you are working on a creative project, place Chrysocolla Crystals in your work area, for example, if you are a writer, place the crystals around your typewriter, computer, notebook. If you are a painter, place the crystals in your paint box or on your easel, on a shelf in the room in which you paint. Place a crystal in a pocket or wear it on a chain around your neck if you are a singer. Chrysocolla works well with the Throat Chakra.

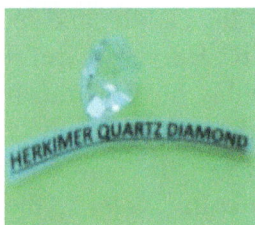

Herkimer Diamond Crystal clears a lot of environmental garbage such as electromagnetic pollution, radioactivity, earth distress. This crystal is excellent to use to help control pain. Simply place the Herkimer Diamond on the impacted area. According to Melody, the "Herkimer Diamond is a powerful purifier." [3] Additionally, this crystal is considered to be an "attunement" crystal and is an excellent choice to have with you during a Reiki attunement,

---

[3] Love Is In The Earth. Wheat Ridge, CO; Earth-Love Publishing House. 1995. P 320

Because the Herkimer Diamond Crystal's energy encourages balance and harmony within the Self, I often use it with clients who are going through a divorce. I place the Herkimer on their forehead at the Third Eye and then proceed with the rest of the healing session. Robert Simmons and Naisha Ahsian in their book, The Book of Stones (Berkley, CA: North Atlantic Books, 2007) support the contention that Herkimer Diamonds are special healers of the emotional body.

Because of their high vibration, The Herkimer may help stimulate one's natural clairvoyance and assist in the development of telepathic skills. If you participate in astral projection or journeying hold a Herkimer in your dominant hand or have one in a pocket or wear one as an amulet around your neck. It is said the Herkimer helps open doorways to other dimensions.

A Herkimer Diamond Crystal Grid provides some unique advantages of a single Herkimer: Amplified energy for purification of environmental and personal pollutants. Here are the steps in constructing your grid.

1. Form a clear and specific intention. Include what your intended focus of the grid is to be.

2. If you are somewhat purest, select a sacred geometry pattern that supports your intention and the power of the Herkimer Diamond Crystals.

3. Your geometry pattern will determine the number of Herkimer Diamond Crystals you will need.

4.You will need an anchor crystal that fits at the center of your grid. This crystal should be complementary to the Herkimer.

5.As you place the anchor crystal, say out loud your predetermined intention.

6.Place your Herkimer crystals in your chosen sacred geometric pattern.

7.Repeat your intention as you place each crystal.

8.Your grid can be left on a table, nightstand, bookshelf.

If you do not have enough Herkimer Diamond Crystals it is acceptable to use other crystals as long as they complement the Herkimer.

Here's a link for a free pack of sacred geometry grids: https://www.mimosaspirit.com/products/free-download-crystal-grid-templates-pack

Sodalite is one of the densest and most grounded of the crystals; thus, making it a wonderful meditation and journeying crystal. Among its several attributes is it brings personal insight; an honest appraisal of one's motivations and it lessens mental confusion. Sodalite increases consciousness and self-confidence. Of all the wonderful things it is reported to do, there is one thing Sodalite does not do. It does not provide wisdom.

Discovered in the early 19th Century in Greenland and again late in that Century in Ontario, Canada, Sodalite soon became a crystal of choice of

support for women. It is said to be helpful for women going through menopause, in coming to grips with the aging processes. If you are oversensitive, defensive, overly anxious, or do things on impulse Sodalite advocates claim it will help you move to a more rational mental process.

According to Judy Hall (The Crystal Bible. Cincinnati, OH. Walking Stick Press. 2003) to block electromagnetic pollution from computers, cellphone, tablets, and other electronic devices, one should place pieces of Sodalite near those devices.

Finally, Sodalite's healing qualities aid in the treatment of metabolism issues, lesson water retention, cleansing the lymphatic system, improving hydration, and the regulation of blood pressure. It is also credited with being helpful with calcium deficiencies, stomach issues, headaches, and problems created by radiation and chemo treatment.

CHAPTER NINE
ALTERED STATES OF
CONSCIOUSNESS

Today people are intrigued by the idea of going into an altered state of consciousness. Their reasons for doing so are widely varied. Whether it is to find a loved one, to try to find a lost will, to locate and retrieve a stolen soul, or to find a teacher going into an altered state of consciousness to journey to another realm is not a parlor game and it has inherent dangers.

At this point, it might be better to identify what science describes as consciousness. Accordingly, consciousness is being aware of your surroundings; the perception of something including your feelings, thoughts, sounds, and your body. An Altered State of Consciousness is a time during which your mind is aware but not in the usual wakeful condition. During this state, you may experience a heightened sense of awareness, a sense of weightlessness, and lightheadedness. Further, at least four features of an altered state of consciousness can be identified: operational, phenomenological, observational, and physiological. Generally operational means a particular technique has been used to alter your state of consciousness. Phenomenological refers to your first-person point of view. Operational involves changes in your overt behavior in relationship to your first-person point of view and physiological is a reflection of patterns of changes in your physical functions.

International author, energy worker, and shamanic facilitator, Franco Santoro nicely sums it up when he states, "What I perceive in everyday life is merely the result of what I have decided to see in accordance both to the consensus reality and my specific role in that context. When I shift my awareness beyond the ordinary mind, then I perceive the world differently." (Trance and Shamanic States of Consciousness published in ShamanPortal.Org. 2002). In 1966 Arnold M. Ludwig is said to have been the first to introduce the term altered state of consciousness. *Altered States of Consciousness: A Book of Readings* by Charles T. Tart was published in 1969. B.B. Walks in his *Textbook of Transpersonal Psychiatry and Psychology* (Kindle Edition, 2009) reports "fully 90% of the world's cultures make use of one or more institutionalized altered states of consciousness and in traditional societies they are, almost without exception, sacred states."

Drug-inducing altered states of consciousness have been around for thousands of years. Today we refer to such drugs as psychoactive, that is they consist of a chemical that changes our state of consciousness, our perceptions, and our moods. The problem with the use of psychoactive drugs is two-fold: the drugs can be habit-forming and second, they can result in your death. Either case is not acceptable. Shamanic work is not necessarily safe and in fact, there isn't any way I know of to make it safe.

Besides the psychoactive drugs, altered states of consciousness can be induced by biofeedback, electrical brain stimulation, vigorous exercise, sensory deprivation, fasting, and rapid eye movements. Continual repetitive behaviors such as dancing, chanting, and drumming can create an altered state of consciousness.

One of the highly touted mixtures that put you into a state of altered consciousness is *Ayahuasca* made out of Banisteriopsis Caapi vine and other ingredients. The word, Ayahuasca means "rope of the soul," a definite indication that there is a spiritual basis for its use. Physical evidence, discovered in 2010 in Bolivia, indicates the use of Ayahuasca at 1000 A.D. What are the effects of using Ayahuasca? Elation, fear, illumination about one's life's task, or a spiritual awakening may result in taking Ayahuasca. There may be negative physical effects such as intense vomiting, diarrhea, or having a hypertensive crisis such as paralysis, stroke, or heart failure.

Not all shamans use Ayahuasca and those who are authentic healers will advise you not to use Ayahuasca unless you are with a trained person and preferably, a highly trained shaman.

At this point, I have to admit to a prejudice about the use of Ayahuasca. First, I have never used Ayahuasca. Second, I do not approve of its use by those seeking to journey to another realm, and third, I do not believe its use is necessary to have a spiritual awakening. Two of my shaman friends disagree with me. One lived in the Amazon for eleven years being trained by a shaman and the other, who does not like to be called a shaman, preferring to render that to aboriginals, was introduced into the shamanic world in Guinea. They disagree with my concern that if one is under the influence of a drug that can make you hallucinate then there is a danger that you will not know what it is that was given to you during your journey to another realm—information often required to help a client heal.

Some claim that their ability to enter an altered state of consciousness brings them enlightenment, Akashic wisdom, and transcendence. These individuals have been viewed with skepticism by scientists who hold fast to the idea that only waking consciousness is all there is and that all others are strictly pathological. I think the biggest contributing factor to this skepticism is the proliferation of "seers," hypnotists, and amateur healers. However, I believe there is a subtle change occurring in the scientific and medical communities as acceptance of supportive medicines becomes more prevalent.

How do you alter your state of consciousness? There are several approaches to go into an altered state of consciousness besides using Ayahuasca. Among these are breathing. One of my favorites is the Ujjayi (pronounced as oo-Jai) Breathing Technique. As with many other areas, each person tends to modify things to meet their style. And that is the way with the Ujjayi Breathing Technique.

Breathe through your nose several times; each time take a deeper breath. Then, place your tongue behind your upper teeth, open your mouth and loudly exhale. It should sound somewhat like the ocean. This may take a little time to get the hang of it. Repeating a specific word as in chanting focuses the mind and opens up the receptivity of an altered state of consciousness. It is perfectly acceptable to use a phrase or even a complete sentence. Rhyming is not necessary. How long you chant depends entirely upon you. Another effective way to create an altered state of consciousness is to meditate. It doesn't make a difference what kind of meditation you do. Experience dictates that anyone can meditate; its depth depends upon you. If you are comfortable with using an empty mind of all thoughts approach and sometimes find you are wandering choose a word to repeat or a number. That will bring you back to focus. Mindful awareness is another approach. You let the thoughts flow concentrating on none. You simply acknowledge the thought and move on. I do recommend you have a quiet place to meditate and perhaps some soft background music.

I want to come back to an earlier statement: Going into an altered state of consciousness is not a parlor game. There are dangers of going into an altered state of consciousness. Participating and practicing going into an altered state of consciousness may induce mental illness in persons who may not be stable. Altered states can open you to the realm of the supernatural and contact with spirits who may not be nice. Hallucinating can result in an individual doing harmful things such as jumping off a bridge, cutting themselves, or setting themselves on fire.

Another issue created by efforts to alter one's state of consciousness is the corruption of one's perception. "Reality tends to be blurred and as a consequence, you may say and do things that deny your normal range of behaviors." (Editor John White. *What Is Enlightenment? Exploring the Goal of the Spiritual Path*. Los Angeles, CA. J. P. Tarcher. 1984, p. xiii.)

CHAPTER TEN
THE SHAMANIC JOURNEY

To begin, I will not be taking you on a shamanic journey during this class. There are several reasons for not taking you on a shamanic journey during this class. Chief among these is that I do not know your physical, mental, and emotional condition. Second, I do not know your physical place, that is, I do not know if you will be leaving where you are and driving an automobile? That's not at all acceptable because you may still be under the influence of the altered state of consciousness and cause an accident.

Sometimes the shamanic journey is referred to as spirit travel or soul journey. By whatever name it is called, the Journey is based on the belief that the natural world has two aspects: Ordinary Awareness and Non-Ordinary Awareness. Ordinary Awareness includes all of your everyday experiences; whereas, Non-Ordinary Awareness is accessed only through altered states of consciousness or during Dream-Time.

People invariably ask me what happens when you journey, what do you see, or what does it feel like? Several answers could be given, but they would have little relevance beyond some generalizations because each person's experience is unique. So much of what is experienced depends upon the individual's intention. There are, however, three general types or ways of experiencing journeying: you have the spirits with you, you are outside of the journey as a witness watching the events unfold, or merging with the spirit, that is becoming one with the spirit be it animal or human, and thus flow within the new Realm.

I want to pause here and talk about intention because it is so very important when it comes to successful journeying and subsequent healing, and that is what I am all about here—healing. According to Webster's On-Line Dictionary intention means "a determination to act in a certain way, a resolve." For me, it is so much more. It implies a decision—a *specific* decision to do something. Please note the word specific. Experience dictates that nothing guarantees failure more than the lack of specificity. How then, do you make an intention? Here are the steps:

1. Choose a specific thing you want before attempting to journey

2. Visualize the process and think about what you have to do to activate that process.

3. Visualize your success

4. Choose a crystal to complement your intention such as quartz, pyrite, carnelian, or moonstone.

5. Add an essential oil such as ylang-ylang, cedarwood, Neroli, or Patchouli to enhance your intention.

An example of a non-specific intention may be helpful. "I want to be well." How might you make that intention meet the specificity requirement? You might say something like this, "I want to stop having frontal headaches." Even that can be made more specific; for example, "I want to stop having the 2 P. M. frontal headaches every day."

As I pointed out in the previous lesson, some healers use hallucinogens and psychoactive drugs such as Ayahuasca or peyote to create an altered state of consciousness. There are other ways of achieving this *soul flight* or *shamanic journey* as the altered state of consciousness is called. Only about 10% of shamanic cultures use drugs. 90% rely upon the drum. (My Path in Shamanism: Interview with Michael Harner from *Higher Wisdom* by Roger Walsh and Charles S. Grob. Albany. State University of New York Press. 2005). Jeff Strong of the Strong Institute says "Practitioners around the world also use chemicals to achieve SSC, [Shamanic State of Consciousness] but I believe the drum and its rhythms provide more control over the latter two components of visualization and ceremony." Even though I have expressed concern over using psychoactive drugs there are at least 5 herbs that help you reach an altered state of consciousness to journey to another realm. As with any plant-based application, you should make sure you have no negative reactions to any of them and that you have consulted with your medical doctor. Lucid dreaming is enhanced by some of these herbs and as such is a gateway to journeying.

Mugwort, a member of the daisy family, may be used as incense, as tea, oil, or ointment. It is excellent for lucid dreaming and helping you shift your focus. It's a good idea to lie down when taking this herb.

Lavender, to help you alter your state of consciousness, should be topically applied to pulse points on your body. Begin with two drops on your wrists, rub them together, and then place two drops on a finger and gently rub it on your throat. Place two drops on a finger and apply them behind each ear. Next, place two drops behind each knee and gently rub the oil into your skin. Be sure you are in a comfortable position, either seated or lying down.

Lemongrass, burned as incense, will help you to shift your awareness, set a mood of acceptance for a change in your state of consciousness. To knock it up a notch, add a single drop of Lemongrass Essential Oil to your wrists, and gently rub it in.

Mexican Tarragon can be used in a variety of ways to induce lucid dreaming from burning as incense, or infused in water as tea. Be sure you are seated or lying down.

Blue Lotus was among the most sacred of plants to ancient Egyptians. It grew throughout Egypt where its consciousness-enhancing properties were well known and taken advantage of. When this flower is soaked in water or wine, and then ingested it acts as an intoxicant. Considered very sacred, the Blue Lotus is used to reach euphoric states of visionary consciousness. It has long been used as a tea and as a smoking blend. It is available as an essential oil. Two drops on each wrist, two drops on the throat, two drops behind each knee and gently rub it in, and two drops behind each ear. Be sure you are seated or reclining when using this plant.

I prefer drumming as the means for introducing the trance-like state that enables travel to the Spirit World. In today's modern world there are CDs, Mp3, and Mp4 files with drumming that are specifically designed to put you in a trance to journey. These also contain a change in a rhythmic pattern to bring you back. The drum I am using for this demonstration is not made of animal skins; it is a man-made material. There will be 4 beats per second.

Please get as comfortable as possible, make sure your clothing is not tight. Take a deep breath, hold it, and exhale. Take another deep breath, hold it, and exhale. One more time. Close your eyes. Normally, the drumming would last ten to fifteen minutes. To end the shamanic journey, the drumming is speeded up. DRUM

Only in an extreme case do I personally journey to seek help with a client's issues. Once in a rare while, I will drum a client into an altered state of consciousness so they can seek the source of their issue(s) and solicit a proposed solution from the Spirit World directly. Sometimes I will take a person on a journey using a CD with drumming created for journeying. I will share one such experience. I have reported this experience in one of my books. I will not reveal the name of that particular book. I do not want to give the impression that this course is for self-promotion and second, I mention this because I do not want to be accused of self-plagiarism.

Several years ago, a young woman in my philosophy class missed a good deal of the semester because she was involved in an automobile accident in which her fiancé was killed. She had spent several weeks hospitalized because of her injuries. She stopped by my office and asked if I would take her on a journey. She wanted to know how she got under her fiancé's body. The police had told her that was where they found her. Within a short time, she was in a trance state. I heard her say, 'Oh no!" and then she began to sob. I turned off the CD; spoke her name to bring her out of her trance. When I asked her to tell me about her experience, she told me she saw the accident and that her fiancé had thrown himself over her, thus saving her life at the cost of his own. A large shard of glass had penetrated his back and severed an artery to his heart. She had suffered several fractures and internal injuries. Sometime later while I was crossing the campus, she saw me and flagged me down. She told me she finally was at peace because she knew what had happened. (Wilson. 2017)

Michael Drake, in *What is Shamanic Journeying?* [4] reminds us that "The key to

[4] (https://shamanicdrumming.blogspot.com

understanding the shaman's world is to realize the universe is made of vibrational energy; that it is a single, flowing, rhythmic being." And I will add, it remains open to be tapped into and that's what transpired with the young woman in my philosophy class.

Vibration is an important key to successful shamanic journeying and healing. Vibration becomes all the more important in today's world of mean talk, bigotry, hate, vitriol, and disrespect. We are bombarded with negativity from TV, motion pictures, and radio. Add to that the negativity that comes from electronics, radiation from microwaves, Wi-Fi, chemical, pesticides, smoking, and junk foods. The healer's job becomes singularly clear: The negative vibrations have to be changed.

There is an inherent problem with our energy flow including those vibrations we are creating as well as the impact from those we are receiving. We say the vibrations are out of sync or there is an energy block. A brief look at vibration will help explain the role it has in our overall health and well-being.

Earth's energy vibration is 528Hz. A hertz, remember is equal to one cycle per second of an electric current, magnetic or sound wave vibration. When your physical and emotional body vibrates at a lower Hertz, illness can result. It is believed that a human body in harmony vibrates between 62-72 Hz. Anything below that suggests an individual has a weak immune system. The shaman's role is to change the vibration of the client; to get it into sync with a natural rhythm.

Certain frequencies stimulate healing. These are the Solfeggio frequencies. I am aware that the term Solfeggio to describe these frequencies is currently debatable. (See Slide 9: See https://roelhollander.eu/tuning-frequency/Ancient-Solfeggio-Frequencies/ for a discussion.) I use the term just as I do the word shaman. It is part of the common language. The significant point here is that the world, the universe is composed of vibration which creates energy. Not all vibrations are at the same beat or resonance. The late Bruce Tainio of Tainio Technology, an independent division of Eastern State University at Cheney, Washington, contributed much to the relevance of vibration. 528 Hz is said to repair DNA whereas, 936 Hz stimulates spirituality, and 432 Hz induces a meditative state and helps bring harmony to the body.

Crystals and essential oils have vibrational frequencies. Rose Essential Oils has a 320 Hz and Lavender Essential Oil has a Hz of 118. Most herbs have a frequency of 20-27 Hz. By adding crystals and essential oils to a healing session in which I use the drum to change the vibrational patterns of a client I do so to enhance the healing processes.

And the phrase, healing processes, brings me back to a very important point about journeying. The primary function in today's world is to help a client heal.

Sandra Ingerman reminds you "It is important to understand as you undertake shamanic journeying that you have complete control of where you go and whom you talk to." (Shamanic Journeying A Beginner's Guide. Boulder. Sounds True. 2004.)

Here are two YouTube presentations on journeying:

https://www.youtube.com/watch?v=i9R2Y6UMbE0
https://www.youtube.com/watch?v=dJG7nQWylf0

Finally, for those of you who want an added boost to making sure your journeying is successful, you may want to consider a blend of these essential oils. They also open the pineal gland. Combine clove, rhododendron, oud, and sandalwood essential oils into a base oil. Use about three drops of each and apply the mixture to your wrists, behind your ears, and the spot between your eyebrows. Again, check with your medical doctor for any allergies, you may have that might be exacerbated by using any of these oils.

CHAPTER ELEVEN
THE SPIRIT WORLD

A brief definition of spirit will be helpful: Spirit is the nonphysical part of a living entity. For the shaman, this includes all living things: animals, plants, the earth. There is an external environment for spirits. It is called a realm. The spirit world is composed of three realms inhabited by good, or evil spirits and jesters, those who love to play tricks on humans. And I must add the spirit world and the natural world are in constant interaction with each other. And because they are, they exist simultaneously. There are at least 10 dimensions. Some today claim there are as many as thirteen dimensions all of which can be accessed.

As I said there are three realms in the Spirit World and it is within the Realms that these dimensions exist. Because you are accustomed to a three-dimensional world you may have to go through some new learning to become comfortable with the multi-dimensional world concepts.

First, a warning; do not equate the three Realms with the religious concept of Heaven, Purgatory, and Hell. They are not the same. Second, do not attempt to go to the Spirit World as you would on a vacation or a grand tour. Third, the Spirit World, like the Universe, does not like generalities, and fourth, you must enter the Spirit World with respect. In this case, a lack of respect means not following the established decorum. And that could cause you irreparable damage.

The first realm, called the Upper Realm, houses Ascended Masters, the teachers-these are the souls of deceased humans. Generally, those Spirits who live in this realm are considered safe for you to interact and communicate with. The Ascended Masters are those spirits who have moved further away from worldly or human attributes, becoming limitless beings. The energy existing in this realm is a direct reflection of the ultimate energy, that which is the Creation.

Some writers now include angels and archangels, and saints as part of the inhabitants of the Upper Realm. These have been added by religious affiliation. For the early shaman, these distinctions did not exist. Human, animal, and plant spirits did exist. Mountains, rivers, and lakes had spirits as did the seven directions; North, South, East, West, Above, Center, and Below.

Because the Upper Realm is a very high-energy place, you may experience a short period of transition when you make your first visit. You may experience layers similar to sea fog as you drive or walk along the ocean or lakeshores, that is, the fog floats in and out. Pockets of light fog might better describe this experience. For the shaman, it is a place of answers.

The second realm is the Middle Realm and it contains human spirits and souls that have not been released. I mean those entities that are still earthbound because their souls have not crossed over. This realm exists within the dimension in which you live. It is here that you meet ghosts and sometimes the souls of loved ones including those of your pets. Again, Sandra Ingerman in her book, *Shamanic Journeying: A Beginner's Guide* states it so very well. She writes, "The Middle World is the spiritual dimension of our physical world." (p.16). It is here that the shaman travels to find lost or stolen objects and like the modern Reiki Practitioner, to do long-distance healing.

The third realm, the Lower Realm, is located in Earth. It is primarily the home of nature spirits, animal spirits, and what is commonly called "lost souls." Their behavior is not always nice, cooperative, or pleasant. Some of the entities that exist in this Realm may exhibit evil tendencies. I define an evil spirit as a soul that has used up its life force by doing bad things to others including the natural world. There is an inherent danger in the Lower Realm. If proper protocol is not followed one may not be allowed to leave as in the Sumerian myth, Gilgamesh and Enkidu, or the Greek myth of Persephone and Demeter.

At this point, it's a good time to talk about protocol. Not following proper protocol can result in physical and psychological harm. For me, protocol simply means those procedures that govern communication. Frankly, I like to say the protocol is simply good manners. In this case, it means greeting the Spirit and thanking the Spirit at the end. Meditate before entering an altered state of consciousness. During your meditation say a mantra that will help stay focused. Offer a prayer to the Directions. Generally, the Four Directions are sufficient. As you say your prayer, offer a smudge of sage or Palo Santo to each of the four directions. Here is the prayer I use. It is simple, short, and contains the secret to getting the cooperation of the Spirit World.

> *Spirit of the East*
> *Where the eye of the Sun awakens*
> *Spirit of the South*
> *Where warmth bathes us*
> *Spirit of the West*
> *Where the Sun closes its eye*
> *Spirit of the North*
> *Where the wind blows the truth,*
> *Grant my request.*

When going to the Spirit World, whatever the Realm or Dimension, never beg, plead, or crawl while seeking help. You must COMMAND. This does not mean being rude or obnoxious. Notice the last line of the prayer, "Grant my request." It is a command, a declarative statement with the subject 'you' understood.

I use this short prayer when I am doing a healing session. I do not speak it out loud. Some clients may not approve of prayer. I also add a line to the prayer: "Bring healing energy to (the client's first name). During this silent recitation, I move in a circle around the client, moving from one Direction to another and letting my body complete a spiral and act as a conduit for Universal Healing Energy.

The reasons for visiting a Realm are as varied as those who take such a journey. Implied here is the fact that not only may a shaman travel to a different realm, so may anyone who is not a shaman. The major reason for a Realm visit is to get help in solving a physical or emotional problem. You may seek advice on what action you should or should not take such as resigning from a position, moving to a new geographic location, leaving a personal relationship, or beginning a new one.

When you seek the help of a spirit do not ask for help in winning the lotto or to do something illegal or immoral. Remember to keep your request clearly stated.

What are Spirit Guides or Helpers? What do they do and how does one get one? Because the shaman connects human consciousness to the natural and spiritual worlds, he or she may find it necessary to use spirit guides or helpers as they are sometimes called. These guides and helpers are also called teachers and often that is their role, to teach you a valuable lesson. And of course, they are here to protect you.

All animals and insects can be a Spirit Guide or Helper. They are with you throughout your life. You may have more than one Spirit Animal and they may come to you at various times in your life. My first Spirit Animal was the great cinnamon bear and I currently have the Bald Eagle which dominates. Each animal or insect symbolizes something. Lists of animals and what they symbolize are readily available. I do caution you not to accept what these lists equate to as the animals' chief qualities. Your Spirit Animal will have a specific meaning(s) to you that may not be on these generalized lists. Do not discredit your sense of the Spirit Animal's power and strength. Do not discredit its reason for coming into your life.

Here are several things you can do to help find your Spirit Guide or to make it easier for the Guide to find you and sometimes they do seek you out.

1.Paying Attention- Paying attention to your surroundings is an easy way to pick up clues about your potential Spirit Guide be it animal, insect, or plant. I like to call this Occurrence Frequency. What animal do you often see? Is it a specific kind of bird, or a deer, raccoon, squirrel for example? This repeated occurrence can be in magazines, books, TV, or movies. It can be in conversations with friends or family. What animal is often talked about? The same holds for plant spirits. What plant are you often seeing?

2.Meditation- Meditation calms you down and opens all your senses to be receptive to visitors. Play soft music; sit comfortably in a dimly lighted room. Arrange to have the TV, cell phone, radio, computer turned off. Use earphones if you have them. Before you begin your meditation make sure you have a clearly defined intention. If you want, you can write out your intention. It might be something simple like this, "I want to meet my Spirit Animal." Next, begin a deep-breathing exercise. You might consider the 5-5 technique. Breathe in, hold for the count of five. Exhale slowly counting from 5 to 0. Repeat this for a few minutes. Then, sit quietly, allowing whatever thoughts come to you to move on, that is, don't dwell on any thought and develop it.

3.Altered State of Consciousness- Altered States of Consciousness can be created by drumming or deep breathing techniques. Again, be sure you have your intention clearly stated.

4.Dreaming-Dreaming can be helped by using Ghost Pipe, drinking Chamomile Tea just before going to bed, or doing a deep-breathing exercise once you are in bed. A cautionary word about Ghost Pipe. This is powerful and should be used sparingly. Be sure you have a certified and reliable herbalist who can make this into a tincture and who can give you correct directions for its use. I strongly suggest you do thorough research on the use of Ghost Pipe before using it. Remember my mantra, check with your medical doctor. Once your dreaming is over, jot down the main points of your dream, making note of any animal or plant that appeared; even if it was but a brief time. Often an animal, insect, or plant spirit will make a brief visit to see if there would be a good match or to see if you would welcome it. You may find Petitgrain Essential Oil helpful. Place a couple of drops along with Lavender Essential oil on a tissue and place that on your pillow or just under your pillowcase. It is calming. Vetiver Essential Oil and Spikenard Essential Oil are both helpful for relaxing and calming.

5.Once you are aware of a spirit entity, welcome it. Listen carefully. You may not be aware of any message until later. If the entity comes back another time the chances are that it is your spirit guide.

Gerald Sinclair in an article,"12 Undeniable Signs That a Spirit is Contracting You," published in Awareness Act (November 14, 2019) mentions three of my favorites: Lights and electrical equipment in your home temporarily seems to go on the fritz, you feel a sudden rush of air when there are no doors or windows open where you are, and you keep seeing shadows move just outside of your line of vision. Generally, and unfortunately, people dismiss these clues as a fluke. Don't do that! As I said, welcome them and listen and watch.

CHAPTER TWELVE
SOUL LOSS AND SOUL RETRIEVAL

Whatever one chooses to call that which transcends the physical body, **be** it brio, élan, prana, life force, or spirit, we recognize that the human being is two-dimensional. By that, I mean the human being has a material body and a non-material body. We call the non-material body, the soul. True, the soul has religious connotations, but it is not used religiously in this module. Abby Stirling[5] points out that Native Americans believed human beings had three souls: Ego Soul which is embodied in our breath, Body Soul which gives energy to our body, and Free Soul which is the Soul that leaves the body during dreams, trances, and travels. Blair A. Moffett supports the idea of multiple souls. He writes, "Much more pertinent are the native teachings that a human being is an entity compounded of several "souls" or aspects of consciousness, and that man and all the kingdoms of life exist and evolve in a multilevel or multiplane solar universe."[6] Shaman of old recognized these three aspects of the Soul and anyone could cause physical and mental illness if it

---

[5] 7 Reasons Why Native Americans Believed Dreaming Is Extremely Important Part of Life. Educateinspirechange.org. August 8, 2017.
[6] Death and the Tree of Life. Sunrise Magazine. November, 1980. ©Theosophical University Press.

should get out of sync. This holds for the Soul when it travels.

Roger N. Walsh in The Spirit of Shamanism (1990 p. 224) reminds us that "the shaman's experience is coherent, meaningful, and consistent with the purpose of the journey." Walsh's statement is an excellent reminder about purpose or intention. The shaman travels to another realm always with a clear purpose or well-defined intention. If she or he did not, the likely hood of finding an answer to a client's problem is nearly non-existent. Walsh further states, ". . . the shaman has good control of his experiences, heightened concentration, and a clear, coherent sense of identity." And that resonates with me since I am opposed to using hallucinogenic drugs.

The fundamental question that needs an immediate answer is what is soul-loss and what causes it? The loss of one's soul can be caused by a severe traumatic experience such as rape, physical abuse and emotional abuse, the death of a loved one, an ugly divorce, an accident, or major surgery. Extended and prolonged pain in some part of your physical body and subsequent use of drugs evolving into dependency may result in soul loss. Sometimes an out-of-body experience, though rarely, can instigate soul loss. A near-death experience might also engender soul loss.

What, then, are symptoms that might indicate you have experienced soul loss? Among the more common symptoms is a sense of being incomplete, chronic depression, anxiety, feeling sad, feeling disconnected from the world around you, a lack of joy in your life, problems in making decisions, or a loss of energy. This list is by no means all-inclusive.

I believe that when you no longer have a clear grasp of what your purpose in life is, it suggests that your soul or part of your soul has been taken away. If your life seems aimless, your daily routine lacks interest, and your social life is lackluster you may be experiencing soul loss. Being a cognitive behavioral therapist, I am aware that in some circles all of this is called dissociative behavior. However, as a shaman, I firmly believe there are other possible explanations; soul loss being chief among those.

Sometimes there may be what is called a *soul exchange*. This means you want to share yourself with another; a child or a lover for example. Generally, this is not a good idea. First of all, it weakens the person giving away a part of their soul, and second, it causes a burden in terms of energy of the recipient because he or she now has additional unusable energy.

Soul stealing is another way by which you may lose your soul. Often, it is not with harmful intent. A mother may keep a piece of her only son's soul when he marries or leaves home. She simply wants to be close to him. In some cases, a mother or father may keep a part of a child's soul who has died. As a consequence, that remaining soul will wander, never finding rest or peace.

It may surprise you that soul loss or losing part of your soul is not necessarily a bad thing. Your soul may leave your body to protect you—protect you from a sense of ego-annihilation; thus, giving you a chance to heal. However, if the soul or its part does not return then malaise may result or a loss of personal energy. In either case, a shaman should be brought in to do a retrieval. The late Michael Harner put it this way: "Our goal in doing soul retrievals is to fill up a person with their self, so they have the energy to create their lives in a meaningful way."

Where does your soul go if you have suffered severe trauma and it has left your body? Tradition tells us that it goes to the Lower Realm, that is, the Underworld. It is here that the shaman journeys and usually with a Spirit Helper to bargain with those who abide there to release the soul or soul part. The soul or a part of it may also go to another dimension. Once the shaman is into trance mode, she or he will have the Spirit Helper to do a location, that is, locate where the soul is.

What preparation should a person do before having a soul retrieval done for them? First, make sure you have checked with your medical doctor that your heart and blood pressure are normal. Second, make sure you have consulted with a bona fide shamanic healer and that there is a missing soul or soul part loss. Third, make sure your intention is clear and specific based. Once these three things have been completed do the following

    1. Make sure you have enough time for a retrieval ceremony and time afterward for a debriefing.

2. Budget private time for yourself after the retrieval so you can process your feelings.

3. Before the retrieval ceremony abstain from all alcohol, sugar products, Pot, and caffeine. The reason for this is these items; temporary energy sources unto themselves may obstruct the shaman's work. That is, these items may generate too much energy.

4. Spend some time out of doors, observe the natural life around you, and observe the sky. Sunrise can be especially comforting as it suggests a new beginning.

5. Establish a specific time and location. Location may be the shaman's office; the client's home, or outdoors. Have someone with you who can drive you home after the retrieval ceremony.

6. Before your session begins, jot down a few comments on how you feel.

What happens during a soul retrieval ceremony? Generally, you would be on a massage table, you would be smudged with white sage or Palo Santo, or a combination. Next, you would be asked to do deep breathing for five or ten minutes. You might be given a Clear Quartz Crystal to hold. An essential oil might be placed on each wrist and behind each ear. The shaman's assistant will begin beating a drum, about two beats per second. Gradually, you should fixate. The shaman may begin a low humming accompanied by the shaking of a rattle. The shaman will then place one hand on your forehead and with the other hold your hand as he begins to journey. Once the shaman has located your soul or its parts he or she bargains for its return and then commands the soul to return. The drummer will stop and the shaman returns to a normal state. The shaman will lean over your head, cup his hands, and blow to transfer your soul back to you. You should remain still, and quiet until the shaman releases you. Then, and only then should you attempt to get up. Spend a few minutes to reorient yourself. There will be a debriefing session and you should jot down a few notes describing how you now feel.

Is it possible to do soul retrieval yourself? Yes, an individual can do soul retrieval on themselves. In preparation, avoid all alcoholic beverages, coffee, tea, sugar for at least 12 hours. Twenty-four hours would be even better. Also, have another individual in the room with you. Before you begin, jot down, on a piece of paper, how you feel.

Here are the steps you need to follow: (These steps assume you do not have a drummer.)
1. Select a place that is quiet and with low lighting. No television, cell phones, or computers (unless you are using it to play a drumming CD or Mp3 file.
2. Sit in a recliner.
3. Have a CD with drumming designed for Journeying. Use headphones.
Have a Shungite crystal to hold in your right hand and a Clear Quartz crystal to hold in your left hand.

4. Have an eye pillow, preferably one filled with lavender. You may use an eye mask in place of the eye pillow.

5. Caution on this one! Be sure you have checked with your medical doctor before ingesting either of the following tinctures. You might want to do a search of these tinctures for more information before taking either one. Take one eyedropper of either Mugwort Tincture or Ghost Pipe Tincture or Blue Lotus Absolute in an ounce of water and drink it about 30 to 35 minutes before your retrieval session begins. Mugwort and Ghose Pipe tinctures help with remembering your dream. In this case, they could help locate and retrieve your soul or its parts.

6. Turn on the drumming and begin deep breathing. Do the deep breathing 5 times and then count to yourself: 0- breathe 1-breathe, 2-breathe 3-breathe, 4-breathe, and 5-breathe.

7. Allow yourself to drift off. If a thought pops into your head, let it be, don't develop it.

8. Gently, repeat three times, "Soul, come home."

9. The drumming CD will bring you back. Sit quietly for a few minutes. Then jot down your experience. You may feel a slight euphoria. You may not notice any difference for a couple of days. For some, it may take a couple of weeks before a difference in feeling is noticed. The phrase that best describes what you should feel is 'light-hearted.'

It is acceptable to repeat these steps; however, I do not recommend doing so more than twice. If you have not experienced a positive change, then contact a shaman to do a soul retrieval.

I have mentioned that someone may keep a part of your soul. This is called Soul Entanglement. In quantum physics, *entangled* particles remain connected so that actions performed on one affect the other, even when separated by great distances. Soul Entanglement is very similar. If one partner in a broken relationship was so wrapped up in the other member, she, or he could have kept part of the soul when the relationship ended, no matter the physical distance between them. As I said earlier, a mother may keep a part of her son's soul as he leaves home. A parent may keep part of a child's soul to protect it. There are entities, spirits, if you will, that are corrupt and delight in bringing harm to others by stealing their soul or parts of their soul. Soul Entanglement, also called Soul Theft, exists when someone holds on to the energy of another so they can maintain their life force. For me, this is corruption.

To get out of the Soul Entanglement do what I call the Fire Bowl." I used it to send intentions out into the universe for manifesting. On a sheet of lined paper, write down the names of those with whom you feel you have a soul entanglement, who are 'energy vampires' and are sucking you dry. Be sure the bowl you are using, can withstand heat from a fire. Cut the names from your list, fold each in half, and then place it into the bowl. Go outside, light the paper and as it burns, say out loud or to yourself each name you put in the bowl and say with each name the following: "I release (your person's name) soul part entangled with mine."

Once this is done, make an offering by burning a Palo Santo stick, smudging its smoke around the area and your body. You can also add a bit of cedar and sage to the fire to provide further protection. Make sure you extinguish the fire.

I am asked how one knows if the soul retrieval has been successful. Foremost, you will physically feel better, even energized. A sense of personal purpose will be clearer. You would have better mental and emotional clarity and because you do, you will establish new healthy boundaries. You will sense a connection to all that is spiritual.

Sometimes a shaman performs a very special function. He or she may function as a psychopomp. Briefly, a psychopomp is a creature, spirit, and in some religions an angel whose responsibility is to be an escort to a newly deceased person's soul to the other side. In such a role, the shaman does not judge the deceased, but simply acts as an escort, a guide. The shaman knows the Realms, knows how to find lost souls, and knows the protocol for journeying in the Realms, he or she can serve as an escort for the deceased individual's soul. The shaman will perform a prayerful drumming ceremony. The vibration created by the steady drum provides a bridge for the soul to cross over to the other side. When the drumming stops that bridge disappears.

CHAPTER THIRTEEN
THE VISION QUEST AND THE
MEDICINE WHEEL

Traditionally, a Vision Quest is a rite of passage for young men entering adulthood. In actuality, the word Vision Quest is a catchall term and since it is an American term, it does not necessarily exist per se in Native American tribes even though many have rites of passage. This sacred process usually consists of fasting for a few days and nights, residing, alone, in a sacred site pre-selected by the tribe's elders. While at this sacred place, the questing individual prays to the Spirits for help in finding his purpose in life and his role in the community. He prays for guidance in how he may be of service. It is important to note that during his stay at the sacred site, the young man remains awake, takes no food or water.

Recent years have seen a spate of Vision Quest retreats, seminars, weekend specials, and spiritual tourism with big price tags. There is an active Vision Quest business today. The tragedy of October 8, 2009, near Sedona, Arizona lingers. That 36-hour stay in a so-called Sweat Lodge cost $10,000 per person and resulted in the death of three people. Caution is the operative word when considering doing a Vision Quest. Unfortunately, these "ceremonies" have little resemblance to the original concept. You can't buy your spirituality or spiritual enlightenment. My purpose here is not to emulate traditional Native American sacred ceremonies. I do not offer Vision Quests as part of my healing practice. It is included here as a means of explanation and of providing basic information. I will, however, include directions on how to go on a Vision Quest that is designed for the contemporary population.

There are several connecting and consistent factors in pursuing a Vision Quest: the initiate is separated from his community, he is housed in an isolated and remote place away from the village, there is complete, and total fasting and that includes no water and continual prayer. The duration of the Quest depends upon the age of the initiate. For a teenager, the Quest may be one day and night and for an adult, the isolation could last four to seven days. Yes, adult males could take a Vision Quest. The fundamental reason for the adolescent going on a Quest is to receive communication from the Spirit World regarding his life's path and to introduce his Spirit Guide/Helper. Generally, the young initiate would receive some personal power as a Spirit World gift, an acclamation of his acceptance.

The first use of the term Vision Quest I have found was in anthropologist Robert Harry Lowe's book titled *Primitive Society*, published in 1920. Vision Quest was used as a way to describe certain ceremonies specific to Native Americans. Maddisen K. Krown (Huffington Post. What is a Vision Quest and Why Do One?) states "The vision quest evolved

142

as a general term that refers to Native American and also to the rite-of-passage rituals found in almost every tradition, culture, and religion throughout the world." [School of Lost Borders. Updated November 17, 2011]. I believe it now is a generalized term that applies to any 'ritual' related to spirituality and to those who seek themselves. I also believe Vision Quest cannot be a group thing. Ayn Rand (d. 1963) stated "There is no such thing as a collective brain; no such thing as a collective thought. We can divide a meal among many men. We cannot digest it in a collective stomach." (For the New Intellectual. New York. Signet Books. 1961. Pgs. 78-79.) The type of Vision Quest advanced here is one in which you take alone and one, in which you do have another human being on standby.

Why go on a Vision Quest? There are as many reasons as there are people. Whatever the reason, it should always be personal, and based on your desire; not on what someone thinks you should do. A shortlist of reasons why you should undertake a Vision Quest includes the following:

1.It helps you to focus on what it is you want your life to be,

2.It will force you to free yourself from all the electronics you connect with daily; the non-stop bombardment of trivia,

3.It will fine-tune your basic senses and tune you in to your physical and emotional worlds,

4.It will generally increase your mental and physical energy,

5.It will provide insight into your spirituality, and

6.It may provide communication with and from the Spirit World.

A Vision Quest may be in any number of formats; from staying in a wilderness area, along the ocean or lakeshore, in a darkened room, in your backyard, on your deck, or a long walk.

There is considerable preparation you should undertake before beginning your Vision Quest. Check with your medical doctor,

1.Abstain from drinking all alcoholic beverages at least two weeks before commencing your Quest,

2.Cut back on the consumption of sugar at least one month before going on your Quest,

3.Increase your protein intake two to three weeks before undertaking your Quest,

4.Meditate fifteen minutes every night and every morning for one month before your Vision Quest. I recommend the Mindfulness approach to meditation.

5.You may want to practice being outdoors in the dark, alone. You can easily do this where you live. Stay just a couple of hours. If you go to a local park bear in mind your safety is always a priority.

6.Make sure you are not on private property without its owner's specific permission.

Several physical things need to be a part of your Vision Quest preparation.

These include basic knowledge of first aid, especially how to stop bleeding and make a temporary brace or sling. You should have a blanket, a small collapsible shovel or plastic poop bags, a large sealable plastic bag for your clothes if you prefer to be naked, and five stick matches in a waterproof, fireproof container. Have a bundle of fringed wormwood sage (Artemisia Frigida) also called white sage.

Because your safety is a necessary ingredient of any Vision Quest, I suggest two modern technologies to have with you; a small flashlight and a cellphone for emergency use only. Be sure a family member or close friend knows where you are and your expected time of return.

You should also have a journal and a couple of pens with you. Record your experiences in the journal. This should include anything you see, feel, hear, or sense.

Depending on your age and physical stamina, the Vision Quest can be from twenty-four hours up to four nights in duration. You are not out to set an endurance record. During the Quest, you are not to eat food or drink water. However, your safety is always your prime concern.

The **Medicine Wheel**, called the sacred hoop, is an ancient earth-based
structure. It was and is used for rituals, teaching, and healing purposes. It may be useful to

some who are doing a Vision Quest. The Wheel is constructed of stones gathered from the area in which the Wheel is to be located. Generally, it is in the shape of a wagon wheel and as the wagon wheel, the Medicine Wheel has a hub and spokes. The hub is called a cairn which is made of a mound of stones around which there is an outer ring of stones. From the cairn, several spokes are laid in and connected to the outer ring. These 'spokes' are also stones.

I have mentioned stones as the construction material of the Medicine Wheel. I will talk about crystals and essential oils as part of Medicine Wheel construction a bit later. Second, in choosing your stones you should take care in their selection. Pick up a stone and if you feel warmth or a very slight vibration choose that stone. If you feel nothing, put the stone back down, and look for another one. You want the stones to be in sync with your vibrations. The size of the Medicine Wheel does not have to be huge as are some of those found in Alberta, Manitoba, Saskatchewan Canada, or those found in Wyoming and Montana all of which were used for community involvement.

Your personal Medicine Wheel can be as small as a foot in diameter. Have it located in front of you, in front of your tent (if you are using one)? Your Wheel can be large enough for you to sit in or lay in if that's what you feel is appropriate. If you choose to sit or lie in the middle of the wheel, you become the cairn. In that case, do not build one.

The exact purpose and meaning of the Medicine Wheel are not known. They have come to be recognized as an integration of the interrelationship between the physical and spiritual worlds. It is easy to step into saying the Medicine Wheel represents life cycles and seasonal cycles including the concept of time itself. Frankly, on a personal level, I believe the Medicine Wheel functions as a symbolic representation of all energy forces; both as a conductor and as a spiritual conduit of that vibrational energy of which all things are composed.

Assume you have built your medicine wheel. How then, do you use it?

First, make sure you have clearly stated your intention. If you have created a Wheel into which you can sit or lay down, do that. Clear your mind and begin to meditate. You can repeat your intention as a mantra to yourself or softly out loud. Once you are calm, begin to make an offering and prayer to the Four Directions. You do this by lighting your sage bundle and smudging it to each of the four directions. Once that is done, be sure your sage bundle is no longer burning. Then offer a prayer to each Direction. If you are standing, turn to each direction; if seated, bow to each, turning when necessary. To the East which represents beginnings and generally is associated with the Upper Realm offer your prayer either silently or out loud. The prayers should reflect gratitude. To the South, the place of growth, you should seek positive physical, mental, and emotional growth; to the West, the place of transition and introspection, you should seek peace in your soul. And finally, to the North, the place of your mental abilities reflective of your survival skills, pray for understanding and patience.

You might begin each prayer with something like this: "Spirit of East", for example," thank you for all your gifts."

I mentioned the use of crystals and essential oils in the construction of a Medicine Wheel. Persons who practice Reiki Healing have begun to set up "altars" that contain a Medicine Wheel. Instead of the traditional Medicine Wheel composed of locally found stones, a small Wheel can be built using crystals. The fundamental shape is still that of the wheel. You may add a four or five-pointed star with each point marked by a crystal. Add a crystal at each cross point. Most Wheels of this nature generally use different power crystals; however, there isn't any reason why you can't use all the same crystals such as clear Quartz, for example. Crystals are from the Earth and in many people's view, have a wide variety of healing, calming, and communicative attributes. You have the choice of placing a small dish containing an essential oil such as Rosemary, Rose, or Lavender at each point of your four or five-pointed star. You may use a single essential oil or a mixture, or a different oil for each point of the star.

148

In the event you have physical or emotional issues crop up during your Vision Quest, do not hesitate to end it and get whatever help you need. Your health and safety are always the priority.

Once your Vision Quest is over, take a couple of days to reflect upon your experience. Because the Vision Quest is such an intensely personal experience, I urge you to keep it that way. Do share with your mentor or 'teacher' seeking her or his insights. Make sure you have updated your journal. Take your time in processing your experience. Sometimes, messages are slow in making themselves known.

CHAPTER FOURTEEN
SHAMANIC DIAGNOSTICS

One of the initial questions I am asked by new clients is how does a shaman tell what's wrong with you? From a shamanistic point of view, there are four areas of potential illness: mental, emotional, physical, and spiritual. And anyone or all of these can be caused by energy loss, sometimes called disempowerment. Stress anxiety, anger, jealousy, low self-esteem, job insecurity, relationship issues, and Soul Loss can cause this disempowerment. Trauma, bullying, death of a loved one, possessive spirit entanglement, or an evil spirit may be involved.

At the outset of an initial client meeting, I try to implant the idea that I do not do the healing; I act as a conduit for the healing energy brought forth by Spirit Guides, Spirit Helpers, and the living Universe itself.

Before the healing session begins, I have the client complete a short questionnaire. Next, during the initial interview, I ask the client for her or his reasons for a visit. While the client is explaining the reason for the visit, I consciously do an aura reading.

The auric colors and their brightness offer a clue to the general well-being of the client. Brown suggests the client is experiencing being unsettled; gray implies the client is having dark thoughts;

mustard connotes pain or anger, and white is an indicator of serious medical issues. After the client is on the massage table, I do an energy evaluation.

An energy evaluation may involve using a dowsing rod or a pendulum to measure the physical energy of the client. Generally, I use a dowsing rod made from a metal coat hanger. I insert the bent end of the hanger into a small piece of plastic straw and then hold it between two fingers. In this way, I am not moving the rod, the client's energy flow is. If, the rod stops at a place on the client's body that suggests there is energy depletion or blockage.

One time when I was giving a demonstration a young woman volunteered to go through a healing. At some point, the dowsing rod stopped at her heart and it stayed still. Someone in the audience said, "Oh, my god. She's got a bad heart." I immediately stopped the dowsing and explained that because the rod had stopped at the heart did not mean she was having heart failure. Then I completed the sweep and after a whispered conversation with the young woman and with her permission, I revealed what the issue was. She had a broken heart and it needed love to repair it. She had had a long-time relationship recently ended.

Other times I use a pendulum to measure the client's energy level. The pendulum may have a crystal at its end or a copper wire pyramid with a crystal hanging inside the pyramid. My preference and this is always personal, is an obsidian arrowhead wrapped in silver. If you want to try a self-energy evaluation follow the following steps:

1.Hold the pendulum between the thumb and your forefinger. Be sure you use your dominant hand. The length of the cord or chain on which your chosen crystal is attached should be about five inches

2.Often a new pendulum has to be trained and at times an old one that has not been used for a while needs to be retrained. Hold the pendulum in your dominant hand as described above and make sure your hand is steady. Ask "Is my name (state your first name)? A yes answer may be a forward and backswing; whereas swaying left and right means "no." A wide circular movement to the right means a "yes" while one to the left means "no." To test the pendulum, ask it if your name is something different than it is. For example, my real name is Norman. I would say "Spirit, is my name Ralph?"

3.Once it is established the pendulum is working, slowly move it up and down your body and then crossways. At any given point it stops moving, you need to do self-healing in that area.

4.DO NOT JUMP to conclusions if the pendulum stops. It may be just a blimp. Wait for a day or two after your self-assessment. If you still have concerns make an appointment with your medical doctor.

A shaman may also use what is called scrying. Scrying also goes by the names of *hydromancy, occlumency*, and *crystal gazing*. It is a form of divination which means to 'foretell.' There are many forms of scrying; among these are wax cloud, mirror, water, oil, fire, and crystal ball. Chapter Thirteen details how to make a Scrying Mirror. Many of the scrying techniques are designed for personal use. Waxing is an easy one for you to use. Get a small bowl about the size of a cereal bowl, fill it with tap water. You will need a candle and something with which to light the candle. Once lit, drip the wax into the bowl of water, let the wax harden. Look at the shape of the hardened wax, seek meaning in the shapes. It may be necessary to seek the help of an experienced shamanic scryer to interpret the wax shapes.

Egg use, not a known shamanic tool for diagnosing a client's issues, is nevertheless an ancient tool for spiritual cleansing; especially in Mesoamerica, a cultural area in North America which includes central Mexico through Belize, Guatemala, El Salvador, Honduras, Nicaragua, and northern Costa Rica. Within this large area of pre-Columbian societies, egg-healing flourished long before the Spanish colonization of the Americas. *Limpia, as it is called in Spanish,* is an easy way to get rid of the physical, mental, and emotional blockage, especially those that harm one's soul such as soul entanglement, bad karma, general malaise, and questionable core beliefs. The egg absorbs energy through the 7,000 pores of its shell which is primarily made of calcium.

Try an egg diagnosis on yourself if you are in a "bad" mood, tired, or lethargic. You will need these items: lavender incense, a white candle, an egg— a more rounded female egg if you are female and a more pointed male egg if you are a male—salt, and a glass of water. Be sure the eggs have been at room temperature for at least three hours. Follow these steps: Fill a clean glass three-quarter full of tap water.

1.Light the lavender incense and smudge the area in which you are located, and then smudge yourself.

2.Light the white candle, making sure it is in a secure holder and will not cause a fire.

3.Place the egg in your dominant hand and slowly move it around your body, beginning at the top of your head. You may roll the egg so it physically touches your body. Do this 4 times. Note the 3 hours of the egg being at room temperature plus the 4 times rollover equal 7 and there are 7,000 pores in an eggshell. For many people, the number 7 is a power number.

4.Once you have completed the body scan with the egg, crack it in the glass of water. Let the egg settle for two or three minutes. Be sure not to move the glass.

Personal interpretation of the results of the egg roll will be quite general unless you have considerable practice. Sometimes, it may be necessary to have a shaman do the Limpia. Here are some of the basic interpretations and as always, if you feel concerned about an issue, see your medical doctor. Look for strings, bubbles, colors, textures, and the location of the egg yolk. Here are nine generalized interpretations:

1.Red spots indicate possible illness

2.Cloudy water indicates mental or emotional confusion

3.Dark spots indicate possible illness

4.A bubble floating on the surface indicates negativity; perhaps negative energy is being directed at you or you are physically and emotionally tired

5.Gray or dark cloudiness suggests you have come in contact with an "evil" eye

6.Spikes or strings pointed downward suggests you have a lot of built-up anger

7.If the water is clear once you have broken the egg and waited the appropriate time, you are fine, safe, and healthy

8.If you see animal or plant images such as an eagle or a flower it means negative energies are leaving you.

9.Bubbles surrounding the yoke indicate good spirits are watching over you.

Journeying which I discussed in a previous chapter can be used in the client diagnostic stage. The shaman uses *transmediumship*. Albeit it is a bit unusual, the shaman invites a power animal or Spirit Guide to merge with her or him in a light trance, and together, they connect with the client's body soul to determine the specific cause(s) of the problem. In doing so, the shaman then knows what to do to help the client heal.

CHAPTER FIFTEEN
THE SCRYING MIRROR AND HOW
TO MAKE ONE
TELLING YOUR FUTURE

We know mirrors have been around for a least 8,000 years. Generally, these early mirrors were made of obsidian and highly polished. What exactly early humans used the mirrors for quite is speculative. Archeologist, Ian Hodder has stated that "one of the most commonly suggested uses is they have something to do with predicting the future or understanding the spirit world through reading images seen in the mirrors." We have examples of mirrors from the ancient Egyptians, Romans, Greeks, Celts, and they were used for spiritual and ceremonial purposes and especially concerning the soul.

According to Wikipedia "Scrying, also known by various names such as "seeing" or "peeping", is the practice of looking into a suitable medium in the hope of detecting significant messages or visions. (01/2022). Those other names include catroptromancy, anthracumancy, and turfumy.

Dr. E.W. Kellogg III, says "whatever one believes about physical mirrors, it makes sense psychologically that dream mirrors may indeed reflect the soul." Continuing, Kellogg says ". . . in addition they may also reveal to the dreamers' hidden aspects of themselves serve as powerful mediums for obtaining important information, and act as useful portals to other dimensions. . .”

What then does a shaman use a black mirror for? It is used as a tool to find answers to questions about the past and the future of a client. However, the function of this video is to set the stage for your scrying. The word *scry* comes from Old English meaning to reveal. It has been suggested that scrying first made use of water. The individual would gaze into a dish of water to see their visions. Most likely you have heard of crystal balls and seen images of an old woman doing a reading.

How do you use a mirror to enter another dimension or realm, or to look at your soul? You will need the following items:

1.A mirror that is 6 to 8 inches wide and stands 10 to 12 inches high. Be sure the mirror can stand securely. If you have a double-sided mirror and one side magnifies, be sure NOT to use that side.

2.Have a candle that is tall enough to be in direct line with your vision so its flame is in alignment with the bridge of your nose. CAUTION: Because there is an inherent potential of fire caused by knocking over a lighted candle while you are in an altered state of consciousness, I recommend using a battery-powered candle that flickers. They are available on the Internet and in local stores.

3.Place the candle in front of the mirror so that when you are seated you can see the flickering flame reflected there.

4.Have a half teaspoon of incense to burn in a fire-proof container, a match, or lighter to light the incense. I recommend a mixture of cedar, Palo Santo, and Copal. A larger amount may be used depending on your preferences.

5.A CD of drumming or an Mp3 file of drumming. Use earbuds if you have them. Set the volume to a moderate level. There are several excellent drumming recordings available. I particularly like Michael Harner's Shamanic Journey Solo and Double Drumming.

6.Sit in a comfortable chair in a room that is quiet, dimly lighted. No telephone, cellphone or TV or pets and family members who disturb.

7.Once you are set, take four to five Ocean Breaths and then quietly say to yourself, "I am open."

8.Allow yourself a good 15 to 20 minutes. Do not be disappointed if your experience is less than you anticipated. The old saying 'practice makes perfect holds here.

Scrying mirrors are available on the Internet and in various metaphysical stores. Prices range from $15 to over $250. You can make your scrying mirror. To do so, you will need the following:

1.A clear glass plate 12 to 15 inches in diameter

2.Matt black spray paint. Do not attempt to use a can of matt black paint. It will run and cause issues.

3.Decorations and embellishments are up to you. If you choose to create a design or images along the rim of the plate us acrylic paint and a fine bristle paintbrush.

The success of your scrying mirror depends on its cleanliness. I suggest using 2 tablespoons of vinegar in a cup of water. Wear plastic surgical gloves to keep your fingerprints off of the plate. Clean the front of the plate first; flip it over and clean the underside. Make sure the plate is completely dry.

Spray on a light coat of matt black paint on the backside of the plate. Keep the spray can at least one foot away from the plate. Spray from side to side making sure there are no pools of paint. Let the paint dry and apply another coat. Do this for a total of six coats. Letting each coat thoroughly dry before applying additional coats. To test if enough coats have been applied, hold the plate up to a light. If any light shines through, add another coat of paint.

Decorate the front of the plate if you desire. Use acrylic paint to add decorations generally around the outer edge. DO NOT decora the interior of the plate.

To cleanse and charge the plate after it has been painted, decorated and completely dried, place the plate, face down on a mix of the following crystals: clear quartz, amethyst, and selenite. Leave it for 24 hours before using it. Follow the procedures previously explained.

A final note: Jot down everything you saw, thought, and or felt during the session. If something doesn't make sense to you leave it alone for a few days. It will gradually become known and understood if there is an intended message for you.

CHAPTER SIXTEEN
HOW ONE BECOMES A SHAMAN

There are a plethora of shamanic practitioners nowadays. The Internet is loaded with websites proclaiming shamanic healing, spirit removal, and shamanic counseling. Even the word magic has been floated around as a descriptor of what it is a shaman does. Shamanic healing is not magic. Courses, weekend retreats, and seminars are offered around the world. I sense most of these are psychology-based rather than sound and plant-based. From my point of view, these courses, and retreats do not a shaman make. They are shamanic practitioners. A PA is not a doctor, but a physician's assistant. Both have value; both are different. The same holds for shaman and shamanic practitioners.

World-renowned psychologist and medical anthropologist Dr. Alberto Villoldo states "The first step toward joining this [shamanism] ancient spiritual and healing practice is typically a calling.[7] A *calling* may be experiencing a strong connection to some aspect of nature; for example, a strong affinity for the ocean, a lake, or a river. Perhaps you had a near-death experience or an out-of-body experience and began an earnest pursuit of shamanic healing. You may have noticed your hands tingle and become warm. Another sign might

---

[7] *How to Become a Shaman*. In Shamanism. April 10, 2018.

involve realizing you could sense things wrong with another individual. This is sometimes called "reading" another individual. Also involved with this might be clairvoyance or clairaudience.

Inherit traditionally meant that a shaman passed her or his knowledge to a novice—a shaman in waiting, so to speak. Usually, this individual is a relative. One of my former college students was a shaman in waiting. His grandmother, a shaman, had begun his training when he was very young. He hoped to be accepted by his community by the time he was twenty. You may pay for training by a shaman who agrees to teach you the healing ways such as the use of herbs, drumming, and how to connect with Spirit Helpers as well as Spirit Animals.

A *Spirit Visit* during Dream Time is another way by which you can become a shaman. The visitor may reveal certain esoteric information. If that is the case, you should contact a shaman to guide you in understanding the information given. Generally, there will be more than one Spirit Visit. Remember, always respond respectfully. If you wake, jot down as much as you can about what you saw and heard.

The Vision Quest which I discussed in a previous chapter could open the doors for you to become a shaman. During this time of isolation, you may be visited by a Spirit Animal who may then introduce you to an Ascended Master. The Ascended then may impart the necessary instruction to be a shaman. The Spirit that may contact you could also be a teacher.

Altered State of Consciousness, closely aligned with the Vision Quest, is a time during which you may receive information about becoming a shaman. You may be directed to contact a plant and herb healer or a specialist in essential oils and crystals. Any one of which, or all of them, could teach you healing methodology. Michael Drake, an international author and recording artist wrote, "Authentic shamanic knowledge can only be acquired through individual experience; however, one must first acquire the methods to utilize them. Once you have learned the basic skills, you helping spirits can provide all the training you need."[8]

Being *Chosen* is one more way of becoming a shaman. This is closely aligned to *Inheriting* which generally means you are a relative. Chosen means you were arbitrarily selected to be a shaman by a shaman. There is an inherent and obvious sensitivity that radiates from you that strongly suggests you are to be chosen. I was *Chosen*.

In 1940, I was on the Baskatong Reserve in Quebec Province, Canada. My parents and I would stay there for three months. There, a MiqMaq Healer initiated me into the world of healing. I met

---

8

https://shamandrummer.tumblr.com/post/136187775238/signs-of-a-shamanic-calling. (Dec. 20, 2013.

her in June and in August, the month of my seventh birthday, she began my instruction.

The learning processes never really stop if you remain open. The number of books dealing with shamanic practices, healing modalities, and the use of herbs, essential oils, and crystals is readily available. The Internet does have its challenge. It is not always easy to get verification of those who claim to be healers, of those who offer certifications, and of those who offer training. If your calling is to help others then the effort is worth it. Namaste.

Also by Norman W Wilson, PhD

Butterflies and All that Jazz with Drs. James G Massey and James A Powell

Windows and Images: An Introduction to the Humanities with Drs. James G Massey and James A Powell

The Humanities: Contemporary Images

Shamanism: What It's All About

So You Think You Want to be A Buddhist?

Promethean Necessity and Its Implications for Humanity

DUH! The American Educational Disaster

The Sayings of Esaugetuh: The Master of Breath

A Shaman's Journey Revealed Through Poetry with Gavriel Navarro

The Shaman's Quest

The Shaman's Transformation

The Shaman's War

The Shaman's Genesis

The Shaman's Revelations

The Making of a Shaman

Activating Your Spirit Guides

Healing-The Shaman's Way

How to Make Moral and Ethical Decisions: A Guide

Teas Soups and Salads

Reiki: The Instructor's Manual

COURSE AVAILABLE

My course, **Healing-the Shaman's Way** is available at Udemy.com. The course is a 17 video-lecture program detailing healing techniques, use of sound, crystals, essential oils, and herbs. Many of the suggestions you can apply to your own healing needs. Here's the link: https://www.udemy.com/course/healing-the-shamans-way/learn/lecture/30410712?kw=Healing-The+S&src=sac#overview.

---

[i] *Linga sharira* is the subtle body within Hinduism's three-body philosophy.
[ii] Science News Feb. 28, 2011.
[iii] Named after German Physicist Heinrich Hertz
[iv] Posted in Metaphysics & Mysticism, November 27, 2015.
[v] If these links don't work, go to YouTube and search for sounds of the earth,

[vi] NAFAS Journey. Shamanic Breathwork May 14, 2020
[vii] Photo from freefoodphotos.com
[viii] an Indo-Aryan ethnic group native to the island of Sri Lanka. They constitute about 75% of the Sri Lankan population.

www.ingramcontent.com/pod-product-compliance
Lightning Source LLC
Chambersburg PA
CBHW051836090426
42736CB00011B/1829